THE SOULMATE PROCESS

T·H·E
SOULMATE
PROCESS

How To Release Blocks & Direct Energy To
Manifest A Soulmate Relationship
Or Transform Your Existing Relationship

———————— ∽ ————————

Bob Lancer

Dedicated to that which is greater than the self.

I wish to acknowledge my wife, Karmelah, for patiently hearing and deeply responding to my work, offering lighted lanterns along the way by which to steer.

━━━━TABLE OF CONTENTS

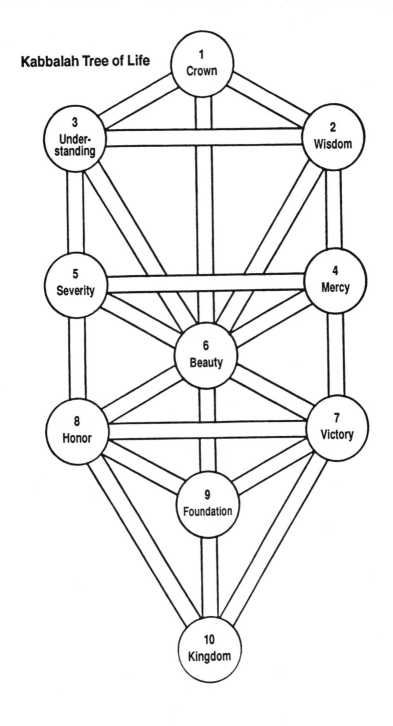

Kabbalah Tree of Life

1 Crown

3 Under-standing

2 Wisdom

5 Severity

4 Mercy

6 Beauty

8 Honor

7 Victory

9 Foundation

10 Kingdom

*"Neither need you worry for tomorrow,
for tomorrow is already taken care of
by the love expressed today."*

—Murdo Macdonald-Bayne

FOREWORD

Your soulmate is the love of your life, the one with whom you can fulfill your highest possible potential while living in the most complete, intimate harmony together, and the love partner you dream of at the deepest level of your consciousness—a level so deep, you're probably asleep to it. The Soulmate Process is aimed at helping you intuitively awaken to your deepest dream of love so you can recognize your soulmate and follow the most direct path into his or her arms.

Soulmate energy is the harmonious field of power that is released and shared when soulmates unite. It is possible to transform any relationship into one that satisfies both with soulmate energy as long as both are willing. The Soulmate Process can take you as far in your journey into oneness as the two of you choose, or *dare*, to go.

It saddens me when I meet people who act as though there is no formula for bringing about the kind of relationship they long for so deeply. To these people, love is a complete mystery—a matter of luck, chance or karma which they must endure like helpless victims.

There most certainly are forces and factors in life that are beyond our comprehension and control. However, there is so much we as individuals can do to direct our love life that there is really no time or energy to spend in fearing the worst or feeling like a victim.

In this book we will explore some of the deepest mystical perceptions of human nature and the subtle laws governing destiny. Each chapter begins with an image drawn from the Tarot. Most people think of the Tarot as a set of strange picture cards used by charlatans to tell fools their future. Those who have seriously studied the subject know that fortunetelling is the most superficial application of Tarot's powerful, mystical symbolism. Each image portrays deep understanding of the human condition in the picture-language of the unconscious. For centuries, individuals have used these images to unlock their greater powers and to awaken higher consciousness.

By meditating on a Tarot image for five minutes a day—consciously observing the details of the card as well as the thoughts and feelings arising in you—you are subconsciously instructed in the wisdom the card represents. To meditate on an image means to look at it consciously, observing the details of the card and also observing the thoughts and feelings arising in you. This simple exercise can result in dramatic changes in one's consciousness, resulting in deeper understanding of life and new ways of living that express higher wisdom.

This is not a book about Tarot; it is a book about you, your love life, and how you can grow to love your life with all your heart. However, you will probably find some key insights into the practical application of Tarot's symbolism. And it is my hope that you will discover a new appreciation for this very ancient system of sacred teachings.

There are also references in this book to points which derive from Kabbalistic thought. Kabbalah is an ancient mystical branch of Judaism that describes the inner workings of the universe and of ourselves. It surfaced in the Middle Ages and its teachings have since been handed down from teacher to student.

In no way am I trying to convince you that there is any validity at all in Tarot or Kabbalah, or for that matter, in anything that I have to say. Everything you will read in this book has worked for me, and it has worked for others. Tarot and Kabbalah are tools that I use to help me see and convey what I know to be true. I have used these tools personally and I have helped others since 1980, using these tools in my work as author, lecturer and teacher of mystical wisdom studies.

This book contains practical tools you can use to direct and learn to trust in your life–specifically, your *love life*. It not only explains what you can do to obtain the love of your life, it also guides you through exercises and procedures for bringing about what you want.

There are also several stories in this book which illustrate others' journeys, challenges and triumphs as they used The Soulmate Process in their quest of love. The stories are based on actual experiences, however, the names have been changed, and in some cases details have been altered, in order to protect the privacy of those whose lives have made their way into this book.

This book represents the light I have found in the core of my heart. May you find in it the guidance that you need as a light through the midnight journey of *your* heart.

Bob Lancer, June 1992
Lake Forest, Illinois

INTRODUCTION ━━━━━━━

The Soulmate Process works. It works every time. It is as reliable as any other natural law. I wish only that I could convey to you my certainty in its working. It is based on the principles by which I have intentionally built my life for the last twenty years, and I have watched one dream after another come true.

You have the power to attract and manifest the relationship of your deepest dreams. You have the power to create your own destiny. You can have the career, relationship, higher consciousness, skills and abilities that you truly want. You can experience limitless abundance. Oh, there may be pleasures you have to forego and sacrifices you'll need to make. There will be suffering because the pattern in your soul requires the growth that comes from darkness as well as light.

But you can have the wonderful, magical, miraculous experiences you long for, if you but dare to dream them first.

The universe constantly and consistently demonstrates natural law. Follow certain steps, and nature responds in predictable ways, but few seem to realize that the same natural laws that govern the growing cycle of all living things also give birth to our life experiences.

Your thoughts, feelings, attitudes, and moods are the natural consequences of the seeds that have been planted, as is your physical health, career, prosperity and spirituality. The same is true of your love life.

A soulmate relationship is the manifestation of your innermost dream of intimate love and harmonious union with another. In the depths of your unconscious, you and your soulmate have already joined. **The Soulmate Process** is a way of applying ageless knowledge and understanding of how the laws of nature work to bring that dream into reality.

There are seven stages or levels in **The Soulmate Process**: 1. Acknowledge the dream; 2. Know yourself; 3. Build your vision; 4. Maintain your balance; 5. Trust what is beyond your control and know that you deserve love; 6. Apply purposeful action; 7. Be true to yourself.

I like to think of these seven stages as the *seven days of creation* of a harmonious love life, and have devoted one chapter to each stage.

When & How To Use the Process

When you work with The Soulmate Process, your dreams of love begin to manifest. If you apply it when you are in a relationship based on love, you will find that relationship progressively reflecting the image you hold in the depths of your soul, which reveals True Love. If you apply it when you are not presently seriously involved with anyone, your love life will steadily improve in line with the soulmate visions of love that you hold.

Every time you apply yourself to The Soulmate Process, you are directing energy into manifesting your dream of love. Whether you work on every phase of the process or one single exercise, your love life will respond by making progress toward your dream. In fact, simply reading this book will bring improvements to your love life, if that is your purpose in reading it. The more time and energy you invest in the Process, the more quickly you will receive its results in your life. To facilitate the process, I strongly suggest you start a soulmate relationship journal to record your thoughts and goals, and to work the exercises in this book.

The Soulmate Indicators

Certain signs are commonly interpreted as indicative of a soulmate encounter, including love at first sight; feeling you have been together before or that you deeply understand each other when you have only just met; the deep, inner feeling that this relationship is destined to be; the awareness that this is the person that you have been dreaming of; tremendous energy which can unbalance you until you develop awareness and wisdom to direct your heightened forces; the sense of a Higher Power bringing you together.

As special as these indicators are, it is not uncommon to meet someone, believe that this is your soulmate, then discover that things do not work out. It is also possible that these indicators will not emerge in your awareness right away. You can be in a relationship with your soulmate for years without realizing it. In any event, by applying The Soulmate Process, you will find more and more of its love and magic will fill your life and your love life will steadily change to reflect your deepest dreams of love.

Tarot Image 21: The World

1

Acknowledge the Dream

To acknowledge the dream of the relationship you desire means you accept or trust that it exists within you. As a result of this trust, it becomes possible to gain access to your inner world and clearly visualize what you want. This does not mean to merely look at pictures in your mind, it means to imagine an *experience* with all your senses.

Imagining Reality

When I was twenty years old, I went to Europe. I played the bongo drums at the time and my friend Steve played guitar. We played in some clubs, in the streets and in parks, mostly in Amsterdam and Paris. My principal objective in going to Europe was to grow as a writer. However, fear and loneliness kicked in and distracted me from my purpose.

I had been involved with someone back in the States, but I ended our relationship before leaving. I wanted her to be free to find someone else because I wanted the same freedom. After a few weeks overseas, however, things changed. The encounters I was having with women over there were not working out. I began to imagine I would never find the right girl, that I had left the best opportunity I would ever have.

I became increasingly nervous, depressed, and insecure. I spent more and more time in the "tea houses" in Amsterdam, indulging in a certain product imported from Lebanon. My dreams of pursuing artistic and literary heights literally went up in smoke. When the trip ended, I felt deeply disappointed in myself for the opportunity I had blown.

As a result of learning and applying **The Soulmate Process,** I became aware that I was experiencing a runaway imagination. I began to accept and trust there was a better dream inside me, a dream of what I *wanted* to happen in my life. I am better able to trust that my love life will follow the direction of my greater dreams. It has also resulted in so many of those better dreams coming true.

Exercise 1: Become Receptive To Your Inner Vision of Love

1. Take three slow, gentle, full breaths. As you inhale, imagine that you are inhaling peace and tranquility while simultaneously inhaling a more alert, awake state of consciousness than you have ever experienced. This state of focused relaxation is called *attention without tension.*

2. Now, state the following affirmation: "Within me is the vision of the loving relationship I want and I can experience this vision at will." As you state these words slowly and clearly, know that what you say is so.

In the Zohar, a Kabbalistic text dating back to the Middle Ages, a mystical version of the story of Adam is told. According to this story, the first human being was androgynous, but had two faces: one male, the other female. The Causal Will behind existence saw fit to separate this double-faced being into two entities. Throughout life, each searches to find the other. The soulmate search ends when they come together again, but this time, face to face.

Adam was feeling lost and lonely. He was unsure of what to do with his life. Looking back, it seemed that he had made all the wrong choices. Recently, he had left his wife of thirteen years to explore the possibilities of a relationship with Evelyn.

Evelyn was everything he had ever dreamed about in a woman. Eleven years younger than he, she had long red hair, large green eyes and a perfect figure. She was outgoing, she loved the outdoors and seemed to enjoy adventure. When they made love, Adam felt as if his greatest dreams were coming true.

He left his wife and son to move in with Evelyn. For three months, Adam experienced a constant high. He felt younger, stronger, handsomer than ever. Although he always felt pain whenever he thought of his son and sometimes when he thought of his wife, the joy of living his dream filled him with courage and raised his self-esteem. He appeased his occasional feelings of guilt and self-doubt by thinking he was demonstrating that each individual deserves to have all life has to offer.

But things rapidly changed. Evelyn began to seem more and more to him like a beautiful but empty package. All the time he had spent perfecting his tan, working out at the gym and going to all the right places to be seen with his new "soulmate" suddenly lost its appeal.

The great high Adam had known was now a dismal low. Every day his spirits plummeted further. He could no longer speak with Evelyn without it turning into an argument. His feelings about himself were like a barren field without the richness of an inner life. Who was he? It seemed that he had lost his values, his integrity ... himself. He even considered suicide.

He wanted to drink away his problems. He wanted something to ease the pain. He wanted to sleep dreamlessly forever.

Then he remembered a white-haired woman he had met in Arizona the summer before. She called herself a spiritual healer. There were many people in the Southwest who claimed special wisdom and power, but she was different. There was genuineness in her eyes. She spoke often of the Kabbalah.

Without another thought, Adam packed an overnight bag and jumped in his Jeep Cherokee. The drive was a timeless period of intense hope and despair. He did not know exactly what was wrong, but a deep, inner confusion filled him with numbing, ice-cold darkness. Eight hours later, he reached Isadora's cabin. The cicadas were buzzing madly, their clamor softened by the song of the creek tumbling past her front porch. Adam looked up at the red-rock cliffs behind her house and uttered a simple prayer. "Save me."

He leaped up the steps and knocked on her door. At first, there was no sound. His heart was pounding and he felt nearly insane. She had to be there. She had to!

Adam raised his fist to knock again, when the door opened. Before he could speak, Isadora took his hands in her own and smiled gently. With the lightest touch she drew him inside. The cabin was simple. There was a large diagram of the Kabbalah Tree of Life on the wall, bookcases overflowing, and more books and papers scattered around the room.

Isadora offered him some tea and asked him to tell his story. He told her he had left his wife and child to be with whom he thought was his soulmate. Isadora laughed loudly at that.

"If you ever actually found your soulmate, you would never know it," she said. "Real soulmates are joined at a level so high and deep that consciousness itself cannot contain it."

He felt ridiculous. Isadora's words burned like embers. She conveyed a truth he could not deny. In his soul, he knew she was right.

"What can I do now?" he asked. "I feel so lost."

"There is really only one thing to do in life, Adam. Focus on your spiritual growth. Each individual comes into this life with a spiritual potential to fulfill. If you make that your first priority, everything else will fall into place—love life, career, prosperity, health, everything."

"But I don't even know what spiritual growth is."

"You will. Just focus on it and you will find whatever help you need to advance you to the next step. The first thing to be aware of is what it is not. It is not your desires, your values, your logic or your beliefs. Stay aware of your inner self so that you can recognize when you are doing things based on attachment to having your desires fulfilled."

"But isn't the desire for spiritual growth still a desire?"

"Yes, but it is the best desire there is if you want to find real peace and happiness. However, even that desire has to be released. Your real Self is guiding you at all times. It is directing your life into the experiences it needs to fulfill its purpose. The more you release to this, the process will accelerate, and the more peace, joy and spiritual healing you will experience."

"But what about that story for the Zohar you told me last summer, about the two faces? How does that figure in?"

"Remember that in the story, the two faces were part of one being. The two entities were lost until they found and faced each other. Then they were joined once again. Your two faces are the two sides of your nature: the personal desires and the real spiritual Self. Your experience has showed you what happens when you follow the personal side of your nature. You're led astray from the path of real peace and purpose."

"So what you are saying is that I have found my two faces. I have faced myself and now I know more clearly who I am."

"Stop resisting the urge to fulfill your spiritual potential, Adam. This urge is what guides and directs you through every experience that you have."

Adam left that evening with many unanswered questions. For instance, it seemed he had made the choice to be with Evelyn based on his desire. Yet, Isadora told him the Spiritual Self determines our experiences.

As he drove back toward New Mexico, he found each question he had being answered clearly in his heart and in his head, as if their conversation had not ended. "If we insist strongly, the Spiritual Self will grant us what we desire, but its only purpose in doing so is to show us clearly that our desires do not know what will bring us genuine happiness and security. That is what happened to me."

Tarot Image 21: The World

At the beginning of this chapter is Tarot Image 21: *The World.*

This image portrays the stage of actualized potential. The wands held in each hand represent mastery of giving and receiving, of intake and outflow. The spiraling ribbon around her represents the awakening of spiritual energy, known in the Orient as the kundalini. The wreath around the dancing being indicates that the ultimate victory has been won in the world—the spiritual quest has begun.

Contemplating this image will attune your consciousness to the true, spiritual path for you. As you hold this image steadily in your mind by focusing attention on it, it can also help you to realize the solution to any problem and the result of any action. Use it in **The Soulmate Process** to help you to release from unbalanced attachment to your desires for a relationship and to keep you focused on what is of greater importance: following your true path through life.

Exercise 2: The World

1. Take three slow, gentle, full breaths. Enter the state of focused relaxation called *attention without tension*, described in Exercise 1 above.

2. Meditate on Tarot Image 21 for one to three minutes. Notice the details of the picture and imagine that the symbol is entering you through your attention and guiding you along the path toward Spiritual Realization.

3. State the following affirmation, slowly and clearly: "I am following the path through life that is truly best for me."

4. You have now completed the exercise. Know that the power within you for spiritual awakening has been set into motion.

CHAPTER ━━━━━━━━━

Tarot Image 0: The Fool

2

Self-Knowledge

Self-knowledge is the basis for intelligent choices, actions and decisions. Knowing what you want in a relationship is an aspect of self-knowledge. To the extent that you accurately know yourself, you can make choices that reflect your actual wants and needs. By looking within, you will receive an inner vision of love that satisfies, excites and inspires you. If your self-awareness is superficial, the relationship you believe you want will only superficially satisfy you. If your self-awareness runs deep, you will know what you need in the core of your being and receive a vision of your soulmate relationship.

Time, effort and a disciplined focus of attention are required to know ourselves deeply. The results, however, are more than worth the effort, because knowing what you want draws it into your life.

The Power To Direct Thought

Thought is a subtle yet powerful force. When you gain the power to direct your attention intentionally, you will be able to direct your life with a level of influence amazing to those lacking this power. This change is not just a matter of belief, but of experience.

The ability to direct your attention consciously is the key to deep and accurate self-knowledge.

Everyone does *not* have this power. So many books and speakers tell us that you can direct your life with your thoughts. But what if you cannot direct your thoughts? When I started to pay serious attention to my thinking I found that it was about 99 percent unconscious, automatic and out of my control.

Like it or not, the fact remains that until one has developed control of his or her attention through training and discipline, one's mind is largely out of control. As long as your mind is out of your control, your ability to direct your life and express your highest potential is infinitely less than if you had that control.

Witnessing your thinking—simply being aware of what you are thinking while you are thinking it—is probably not your habit, which is why it needs to be practiced intentionally. Generally, people assume they are already doing this until they actually begin to work at it. Though it may at first seem like a hopeless task, by sticking with it, the power to consciously control and direct our thoughts grows.

By witnessing thoughts and feelings, they begin to clarify. You leave the levels of superficial knowledge behind and make your way into the depths of self. One fear that keeps us from doing this is the fear of discovering and having to face the pain of dissatisfaction that may have been secretly lurking there all along. But there is nothing to fear because when you know what you long for you can begin doing things to bring it into your life.

Knowing what you want in a relationship is as much your responsibility to yourself as it is to your partner. When we expect others to understand us better than we understand ourselves, it is easy to become frustrated and blame them for our dissatisfaction. However, as we become more clearly aware of what would fill us with joy, peace and love, we empower ourselves to make better choices and we increase the likelihood that our lover or mate will recognize our feelings and willingly support our happiness.

Becoming clearer and more precise in our awareness of our wants occurs through the intentional practice of self-awareness applied over time. Even if you are not in a relationship, this is useful because it will help you to intuitively sense the individuals who are aligned with your needs and to make choices in general that are more aligned with your love life goals.

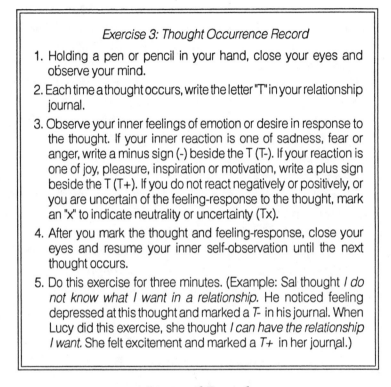

Exercise 3: Thought Occurrence Record

1. Holding a pen or pencil in your hand, close your eyes and observe your mind.
2. Each time a thought occurs, write the letter "T" in your relationship journal.
3. Observe your inner feelings of emotion or desire in response to the thought. If your inner reaction is one of sadness, fear or anger, write a minus sign (-) beside the T (T-). If your reaction is one of joy, pleasure, inspiration or motivation, write a plus sign beside the T (T+). If you do not react negatively or positively, or you are uncertain of the feeling-response to the thought, mark an "x" to indicate neutrality or uncertainty (Tx).
4. After you mark the thought and feeling-response, close your eyes and resume your inner self-observation until the next thought occurs.
5. Do this exercise for three minutes. (Example: Sal thought *I do not know what I want in a relationship.* He noticed feeling depressed at this thought and marked a *T-* in his journal. When Lucy did this exercise, she thought *I can have the relationship I want.* She felt excitement and marked a *T+* in her journal.)

Lost and Found

Calvin and Marci had been high school sweethearts. Their relationship continued throughout four years of college even though they went to schools in different parts of the country. Following graduation they married.

Calvin seemed to love Marci very much. It was obvious to everyone that knew them that he did whatever she asked. He never seemed angry and never raised his voice.

His endless accommodation elicited Marci's trust in him to the extent that it was not difficult for her to admit to him one evening that she was having an affair.

Calvin did not know how to respond. He thought asking her

to stop seeing the other man would be selfish. He blamed himself for her need to go outside the relationship, but he was careful not to show her how he felt because he did not want to make her feel bad. Not knowing what to say or do, he asked if she planned to continue the affair, "or do you want me to leave so you can be with him?"

One might have thought that this would have touched Marci's heart and made her feel that she was married to an angel. But it infuriated her. She shouted at him, "Aren't I worth anything to you, Calvin? Aren't I worth anything at all?"

He just looked at her.

"Aren't you going to say something?"

He spoke as evenly and gently as he could, hoping that it was the right thing to say. "Do you want a divorce?"

"God damn it, Calvin. What the hell do *you* want?"

"I want you to be happy, Marci. That is all I've ever wanted."

"But what about *you*? What makes *you* happy? Don't you think that I need the joy of making someone happy, too?"

Tears filled his gentle, brown eyes. A large man, Calvin strongly resembled a big, sad teddy bear. "I don't know," he sobbed.

Marci was not interested in her affair. Until that instant she hadn't even known why she was doing it. But now she understood. It was a ridiculous attempt to elicit some emotion, any emotion, from Calvin. If she had been consciously aware of her motivation, she would have chosen a better way. Now that she knew what she was trying to accomplish, she tried another approach. She asked Calvin to find out what he truly wanted in a relationship. He agreed.

For the next few months, he kept a daily journal. At the end of each day he recorded what happened that day between Marci and himself. Next to the things that occurred which he found pleasant or desirable, he put a check. Next to the things that occurred which he found unpleasant or undesirable, he put a minus sign. When his feelings were unclear or neutral, he indicated this with a dot.

This was not easy for Calvin, but he disciplined himself to do it until he built up momentum. He began to find that there was something satisfying in this exercise.

As Calvin progressed in this work, he seemed to become a different person. He not only *found* himself, but he also found the courage and self-esteem to *be* himself. He became more assertive in his relationship with Marci, not because *she* wanted it, but because *he* needed to express himself. And Marci was delighted because, as he came to know himself, she came to know who she was with.

Love Life View

In your journal, describe your current love life situation. Do not judge or analyze, just describe it as the thoughts and feelings occur to you. This reveals the value of self-knowledge as a power for directing your love life. For instance, Meg wrote the following paragraph describing hers:

"Periodic arguments which become rather intense. Sometimes it seems that he is my soulmate and I find myself thinking that I love him so much. Our lovemaking is so erotic. He seems too possessive at times, yet other times he seems so understanding. I hope that we do not fight again soon. I want to remain calm and emotionally balanced when he loses control, or is out of my control. We seem to have a conflict over money."

Gary, who was not in a relationship at the time, described his relationship this way: "Loneliness. Wishing I had someone to share my life with. Wanting sex. Feeling strongly attracted to Julia, but I don't think she feels the same way about me. Want to be patient so that I make the right choices. I feel sometimes that my limited income makes me less desirable or even unworthy, seeing as how I have less to offer. Need more discipline to keep my apartment neat and clean."

Once you have described your current love life situation, you will probably feel clearer about it than you were before you wrote it. Writing about something helps us to concentrate on the specific details of it, and that leads to clarification, which almost always brings increased peace, security and confidence. As you become more aware of *what is*, you will find a clearer sense of direction guiding you toward making things better.

You can take this exercise a step further by indicating the way you feel about the factors of your situation. Place a check beside those aspects or conditions which you find desirable, and an "x" beside those which you find unpleasant or would rather avoid. When your feelings about a condition are neutral or unclear, leave a dot to indicate that.

Response-Ability

Focusing on my response to a person, place or event rather than the stimulus itself frees me from being the victim of my circumstances. I am able to improve my response for better results. This is especially helpful when I am upset, impatient or angry. I do not have to feel the way that I do. The pain of my reactions is caused by my reactions. This stops me from blaming and involves me in the process of changing my response.

Exercise 4: Focusing Attention On Your Response

1. State the following, slowly and clearly: "I am aware of my responses in the now."
2. Follow the affirmation with thirty seconds of self-observation. Simply focus awareness on yourself.
3. At the end of thirty seconds, repeat steps 1 and 2.
4. Do this for three minutes.

Another way to work on your responses that is specific to your love life is to describe your current love life situation in just ONE word. Label a page in your journal "One Word Descriptions" and write the first word that comes to you which seems to fit. For example, a woman named Anna wrote down the word *division*. The thought she had was that she and her boyfriend did not blend harmoniously. On some level, they were like oil and water. Periodically, you can refer back to this page and update your responses.

Writing just one word to describe things helps us to simplify our focus and identify key elements. Once you have written that word, notice your response to the condition it represents. Does it sadden you, please you, make you angry, ignite your impatience, fill you with hope, make you feel tired or depressed?

Whatever your response to the situation, take responsibility for it. A wise person once said, "Control of circumstances begins with control of your reactions to them." This exercise is aimed at helping you to gain an important element of self-knowledge: how you respond to your love life.

Once you are aware of your response, ask yourself how well it is working for you. If it is empowering, constructive and harmonious, keep it. If not, work on it. Open your imagination to a different response that would work better. If one does not occur to you right away, be patient and trust that it will.

Commitment

Rollins was a successful attorney. In his late thirties, he owned a Porsche, a ski villa, a condo, and several investment properties. He also paid alimony and child support from two divorces.

He had made a lot of money, but every seven years it seemed that he was starting over. He was drained on other levels as well. Leaving his children was the hardest thing he had ever done.

He believed that he had a commitment problem. The marriages he left were happy and the women had been his friends as well as his lovers. But his relationship pattern was too strong.

Whenever he became comfortable and secure in a relationship, he was beckoned by the allure of a sexy stranger and he longed for the excitement a new relationship seemed to promise. Enamored with the thrill of the chase, his eye would roam, then his thoughts, finally his body.

He and his latest girlfriend, Viki, were living together. Things were just beginning to get comfortable. One day at work, a secretary winked at him and he found himself flirting with her. Later, he thought about his relationship with Viki and realized he was beginning to feel stifled. He examined the feeling and discovered that he was comfortable with Viki; they made a good team, and he was happy with her. Then why the urge to chase other women? Rollins was upset. He did not want to have to go through this any more. He was tired of letting others down. He wanted to know what a committed relationship was like.

In search of an answer, he practiced self-awareness. While observing his responses, he had a revelation. He realized he'd been associating the excitement of romance with having an affair. This was a mental concept that he had been unconsciously identifying with for years.

He began to focus on fulfilling his needs for excitement *and* commitment into a single love goal. He made plans that he and Viki could share—trips, new experiences, new risks—and was overjoyed when she reacted eagerly. He discovered new sides to Viki as well as himself. As their love grew, so did their romance. Rollins had broken through unconscious, destructive thought patterns and was free to enjoy a lasting, committed relationship that never lost its excitement.

Tarot Image 0: The Fool

We began this chapter on self-awareness with Tarot Image 0: *The Fool*. It represents the element of trust we all must have in the Higher Power that rules the universe.

The individual pictured is apparently about to dance off a cliff. However, he does so with a trusting look on his face. He gazes up toward the Higher Power that rules rather than downward where his body is doubtlessly headed. This portrays the fool's transcendence of the natural instincts for survival. The dog faithfully following him, on two legs instead of four, also represents the metaphysical energy which liberates us from matter.

Obviously, the individual is foolish when considered from a

practical perspective. However, maybe not. We all must be willing to release ourselves from attachments. The universe is stronger than we are. It takes things from us and gives things to us seemingly against our will. The Fool represents our power to trust that Higher Power instead of fearing it.

Zero is a limitless number and a fool is one who believes in limitless possibilities. Lacking the knowledge and experience of those more "wise," the fool also lacks the expectations and limiting beliefs based on logic and past experience.

The Fool represents the deepest level of self-knowledge portrayed by the Tarot. It points to that level of ourselves which is connected with the infinite.

Use this image to re-ignite the infinite element in your soul, as well as to develop your trust. When you meditate upon this image as part of **The Soulmate Process,** it helps you accept your love life positively, as an adventure of unlimited possibilities. The image will subtly burn away the subconscious attachments which unbalance you and hold you back.

Exercise 5: The Fool

1. Take three slow, gentle, full breaths and enter the state of focused relaxation called *attention without tension.*

2. Meditate on Tarot Image 0 for one to three minutes. Simply look at the details of the picture and imagine that the image is entering you through your attention. Try to feel the image impressing itself on the core of your being. As you breathe in, imagine the image and its power filling you. Imagine the picture is inspiring you through the impact of its imagery to fulfill your spiritual potential.

3. State the following verbal affirmation three times, either silently or aloud: "I am trusting and at peace with the limitless power at work in my life."

4. Having stated this affirmation, know that The Fool within you is now set free to fulfill *his* purpose, which is to open *you* to the limitless possibilities of yourself and your love life.

CHAPTER

THE MAGICIAN.

Tarot Image 1: The Magician

3

Build The Vision

It is a well-known fact that magnetic fields attract. This applies in human relationships just as much as it does in physics. Those people who come together in life have attracted one another.

It is common to think an individual is attractive because of personal qualities. He is handsome, she is pretty; he has a great personality, she is kind and caring; he is sensitive, she is down-to-earth. However, there is another level of attraction between individuals which has a stronger influence than personalities, appearances and possessions. It has to do with the dynamics of energy and the polarity of power.

You can direct what you radiate in order to attract the relationship you desire.

If you are not presently in a relationship, there is someone out there you long to be with. If you are in a relationship, there are ways you and your partner can grow and change in order to progressively fulfill both person's needs for soulmate energy, while each fulfills his and her own individual life purpose. One of the ways to attract the experiences you want is by directing what you radiate. Anyone who wants to can learn how this is done.

Thoughts and feelings radiate from us in the same way our speech and actions do. Others are affected by the way you think and feel. This is particularly true when you are thinking and feeling about *them*.

If you observe your relationships carefully, you will begin to see that your thoughts and feelings have a definite impact. Others somehow pick up and respond to our inner states. Business people who secretly resent their customers can find definite changes for the better by disciplining their feeling and thinking along these lines. There is a well-known story of a great actress who understood the power of thought and feeling in relationships. Before each stage performance she would spend one hour in her dressing room thinking of the audience with the deepest love and compassion she was capable of.

What you think and feel about *yourself* also affects you. If you think of yourself as inadequate, inferior or worthless, you act in ways that reinforce those beliefs and continually feel depressed, defensive, and resentful. I observed this principle in action repeatedly with "difficult" students when I worked as a high school English teacher. By focusing on the students' strengths rather than weaknesses, they would begin to feel better about themselves, which always resulted in better classroom behavior and better performance overall.

There is a saying that what you condemn in yourself or others you condemn yourself to repeat. If you are angry with yourself or others, you are likely to find that you continue to do the things you want to *stop* doing or avoid, and continue *not* to do the things you would rather experience instead.

This same principle applies to your love life. If you think, feel or expect what you do not want to happen, that is what is bound to continue. If you fill your head, for example, with the idea that "relationships don't work," or "there are no marriageable men out there" because you read it in the newspaper or your friends feel that way or your mother said it was true, then it becomes what you radiate and is what you will receive back.

Negative thoughts and feelings can produce a thick screen around us which our potential soulmate cannot see through and therefore cannot recognize who we truly are. It can push away from us the very experiences we desire most to have happen in our love lives. However, there is a way out. You can direct what you radiate to attract the consequences you design.

The people around us radiate their innermost thoughts and feelings. If you find yourself feeling inadequate, depressed, hopeless or insecure around certain people, it might be because they are feeling that way and you are receptive to their inner states. Just being aware of the possibility that this could be happening has helped me to become less identified with and stuck in the thoughts and feelings that work against me.

Creative Attunement

You cannot be attracted to something that does not exist. As long as you are looking for a mate, you can be sure that the mate you are looking for exists. The moment that you desire something, it begins the process of manifestation in your life.

Whatever you focus attention on is where your life is headed. By directing your attention to the experience that you want to have, you radiate the necessary vibratory pattern to draw that experience to you. You become open and receptive to its manifestation in your experience.

The following exercise is a means of directing your attention into the energy patterns of your soulmate relationship. By focusing on the energy of your union with your soulmate, you are tuning into soulmate energy and drawing the relationship experience you want into your life.

If you notice some resistance to this practice because it is difficult to accept that you can unite with the love of your life, keep at it. Gradually, your barriers to true love will give way.

After a period of steady, daily practice, people usually find that they have built a constant source of strength and belief in their greatest dreams coming true. You know the feeling you experience when you have fallen in love with someone who is in love with you? It not only fills you with confidence, self-esteem and compassion for others, it also makes you naturally more attractive to others. This exercise will release that feeling.

The more you practice the exercise, the more this feeling is strengthened until nothing can shake your confidence and belief in the most joyous possibilities of life.

Exercise 6: Creative Attunement

1. Stretch your body and take a few long, relaxing breaths and enter the state of *attention without tension.*

2. Imagine now that you and your soulmate are holding hands and gazing at one another. Make no attempt to make out the physical details of your soulmate. Focus only on the inner feeling of your closeness.

3. Continue to imagine that your desire for complete physical, emotional, mental and spiritual harmony with one another is fulfilled.

4. As you breathe in, imagine that you are breathing in the energy of your soulmate's presence and your harmonious union.

5. Imagine now that your innermost self, your spiritual self, is letting you know that this is the relationship that you were meant to have, in line with your spiritual destiny.

6. As you continue to focus on the energy of your union, state the following affirmation slowly and clearly three times: "I and my soulmate are one."

7. Experience the uncontainable joy of knowing that you are completely satisfied with your soulmate relationship on every level: physical, emotional, mental and spiritual, and feel the relief that comes with knowing you are finally united.

8. Finally, experience the luminous radiance of your loving union as the heartbeat of the universe, spreading out and traveling throughout the world as the healing light of love.

9. Continue your focus on the experience of soulmate energy for three minutes, or longer if you like. This feeling of harmonious union with your soulmate empowers the attraction which draws the two of you together.

Spend as much time as you like doing this exercise. Eventually it will become easy to do at any time.

The Soulmate Chart

On a clean page in your Relationship Journal, draw an equilateral triangle pointing up. Label the top angle "Relationship Between," the bottom left angle "Self," and the bottom right "Other." This triangle portrays the three fundamental elements of a soulmate relationship: *self, other* and *the relationship between the two,* which in a soulmate relationship becomes the soulmate *Flame of Love.*

On the next page in your journal, make three columns. Label the left column "Self," the middle column "Relationship," and the right column "Other." Along the left of the page, number from one to ten.

In the ancient mystical wisdom system called Kabbalah, ten is the number of physical manifestation. Kabbalah is rooted in a deep understanding of the subconscious mind. By incorporating its number system here, you can give yourself additional mystic energy in the process of manifesting your soulmate relationship.

Before beginning, center yourself with the breathing exercise and enter the state of *attention without tension* as described in Exercise 1 on page 12. State this following affirmation slowly and clearly: "I am vividly aware of the loving relationship experience I want." Close your eyes and imagine that you and your soulmate are together, sitting face to face (or in any other scene you prefer). Focus on the inner feeling of your being together in perfect harmony.

Next, under the *Self* column, list ten desirable conditions or qualities that you imagine yourself expressing or exhibiting in the relationship you want. In the *Other* column, list ten qualities or conditions that you want or imagine in your soulmate. In the *Relationship* column list ten qualities or conditions that pertain to the way you want the two of you to relate.

Explore your own heart and mind when it comes to each one of these elements. In the final analysis, it is really up to you as to what a soulmate relationship is. It is, or can be, whatever you want it to be. It is the relationship that satisfies every level of your being. This exercise is your opportunity to create the kind of relationship that fulfills your deepest dream of love and is in line with the Will of your innermost self.

I recommend that you take this list quite seriously. Approach it as the architect of your destiny. It is a means through which to build the abode of your spirit in the future.

Here is a sample of my three lists:

Self: Happy, smiling, relaxed, grateful for the past, the feeling that this is right for me, independent, feeling free to follow my true way, healthy, the feeling that my career is in harmony with the relationship, the feeling that she and I have always been destined to be together.

Other: Faithful, non-smoker, likes outdoor activity, intelligent, artistic, open-minded, kind, respects my spiritual nature, thinks for herself but can listen to my point of view with an open mind, truly loves me deeply.

Relationship: Respectful speech, deeply satisfying lovemaking, sincerely romantic, in harmony with career and material success, in harmony with maximum spiritual growth, interdependent, lifelong, adventurous yet practical, energetic and youthful, compassionately serving the world.

The list which some find a little abstract at first is the *Relationship.* This pertains to the qualities of the relationship itself. Focus on what is transpiring between the two of you and break it down into ten aspects, qualities or conditions. Another way of thinking of this is in terms of "us." What can you say about "us" in your Soulmate relationship, or "we"? Those are the qualities to list under this heading.

Another way of understanding what to write is to begin by saying to yourself: " I am ..." or "I do ..." under the *Self* heading; " He or she is ..." or "He or she does ..." under the *Other* heading; and "We are ..." or "We do ..." under the *Relationship* heading.

When you are clear on what you want and let the universe

know what it is, it locates the composite and sends him or her your way. Remember, you cannot be attracted to something that does not exist. As soon as your desire becomes conscious, it is a foreshadowing of the opportunity for its own fulfillment.

If you are finding it difficult to come up with ten details, you may be trying too hard. Treat your first attempt as a rough draft. You may not be entirely clear about exactly what you want. Simply write ten things however hazy, uncertain or superficial they might seem. If you cannot come up with ten right now, come as close to that number as you can.

You may find it helpful to think of past relationships you have experienced or observed. Think of other people that you have admired or found desirable; those can suggest to you the qualities which you would like to have in a mate. Can you recall relationships which demonstrated the kind of harmony you would like to have? Can you remember past relationship experiences in which you exhibited something like the qualities you want to exhibit again?

If you choose to use the past consciously in this manner, avoid projecting the actual qualities that you have seen. Use the past to indicate types rather than particulars. For example, if someone spoke in a voice you liked, don't focus on that particular voice; focus on that *type* of voice.

You may find it easier to imagine these in a different order. For instance, you may prefer to first imagine the qualities you want in your relationship, then in your mate and finally to imagine your pleasant response to these. Choose the sequence that is easiest for you.

Return to this list once a day to revise, refine and update it. It is also useful to rewrite it. Because writing involves the body, it sets the momentum of physical energy in motion, which makes it easier to act in ways that are aligned with your love goals. Writing also deepens the concentration of attention and that sends greater power into the process.

Each time you do this exercise do not focus on the words as if they have a power of their own. Rather, treat the words as symbolic tools which help you to focus on the inner, imaginary experience which they label or represent. This will result in your imaginary view and feel of your soulmate relationship becoming stronger, clearer and more meaningful. As this happens you are attracting to you a future that more deeply and precisely harmonizes with your true being.

The Five-Level List

Here's a variation on the **Soulmate Chart** you recorded in your Relationship Journal. This variation breaks the soulmate relationship into five levels: physical, emotional, mental, spiritual, and social. In reality, these levels cannot be separated. As long as we are alive, all five levels are inherently connected. However, by focusing on them individually, they become guidelines for constructing and attracting a balanced relationship that harmonizes on all levels.

The five-pointed star is a very ancient, very powerful symbol of the human being. On the next page in your journal, I want you to draw a five-pointed star. You can do this freehand or trace a pattern. Maybe you think you're not an artist, but it doesn't matter how perfect the image is—the physical energy you put into the drawing is what empowers it.

Label the top point "Spiritual," the top left "Mental," the bottom left "Physical," the top right "Emotional," and the bottom right "Social." Label the middle "Being."

On the next page, make three columns. Label the left "Self," the middle "Relationship," and the right "Other." Along the left side going down, mark off five sections and give them the same labels as the five points of the star.

Before beginning to fill in the columns, center yourself with the breathing exercise and enter the state of *attention without tension* as described in Exercise 1 on page 12. State this following affirmation slowly and clearly: "I am vividly aware of the loving relationship experience I want." Close your eyes and imagine that you and your soulmate are together, sitting face to face (or in any other scene you prefer). Focus on the inner feeling of your being together in perfect harmony.

In the *Self* column, under the word **Physical,** write a physical quality, mannerism, condition or activity that you observe in yourself, such as: I am physically healthy.

Under the *Other* column do the same. For example: he (or she) has gentle eyes.

Under the *Relationship* column describe a physical quality, mannerism, condition or activity that you engage in together. For example: we are holding hands.

Next, go down to the emotional level and follow the same sequence. For example, for yourself you might write: The sense of relief that we are finally together. For the other you might write: he (or she) loves me deeply. For the relationship, describe the emotional atmosphere between you, such as: loving, sexual, friendly, peaceful, happy, etc.

Do the same for the mental level. About yourself, you might write: feeling intellectually sharp or stimulated. For the other: capacity for deep understanding. For the relationship, describe the intellectual atmosphere between you or the way that your intellects match; for example: intellectual equality, ability to understand each other, clear communication, etc.

Do the same for the spiritual level. For yourself, you might write: knowing that this relationship is aligned with my spiritual being. For the other: accepts and understands my spiritual values and concerns. For the relationship, describe the way your spiritual levels interact, such as: spiritual harmony radiates from our relationship, supportive of one another's spiritual path, both equally interested in spiritual issues, etc.

Finally, do the same for the social level. This level pertains to how the two of you relate with others, or the rest of the world. For yourself, you might write: comfortable with others. For the other you might write: he (or she) is satisfied with the relationship and feels that way when relating with others. For the relationship, describe how your relationship affects others and how you relate with others as a couple. For example, you might write: others are comfortable around us, we are mutually dedicated to social issues for the betterment of mankind, we attend seminars on personal growth, etc.

Extend this list to as many qualities under each heading as you can, but stop at ten for each. As with the previous chart, do this one regularly. Return to it to revise, refine and update it. As you go through experiences and over time, your goals for a soulmate relationship will change, deepen and clarify. It does not matter which **Soulmate Chart** you use the most. What does matter is that you use at least one of them regularly to continue to direct your love life into your deeper dreams.

The **Soulmate Charts** are helpful in setting into motion the inner vision of the love life experiences that you want. In addition to using the chart exercises, practice focusing on your vision of love during daily life. Every so often, simply imagine the soulmate experience that you want. If your vision and feel of the experience is faint and vague, that is fine. If you do this, say, five times during the day you will find that your inner vision becomes progressively more vivid.

The more attention you devote to the inner knowing, feeling and vision of the soulmate experience that you want, the more energy you send into the process and the more quickly progress is made in your love life.

Spend the next sixty seconds focusing inward on your soulmate vision now.

There is nothing too superficial for your **Soulmate Chart**. Nothing that you find attractive is unworthy or impossible (as long as it does not involve taking advantage of another's vulnerability or infringing on another's free will). If your desires seem contrary to your deeper values, suppressing them or condemning yourself will not make you a better person. Face your conflicts and resolve them in a healthy, compassionate way that works.

Soulmate Illusion

It is possible to meet someone and be thoroughly convinced that this is your soulmate. As you come to know the person better, you may find out that you were mistaken. There are many reasons for this. It may be that this individual pressed certain buttons, consciously or unconsciously, that triggered your "this is my soulmate" reaction. It may be that, due to an unbalanced emotional state, or a state of wishful thinking, you saw what you wanted to see.

The protection from this kind of disappointment is to remember the principle of non-identification. This is the principle of not identifying your inner, soulmate visions with any particular person that you know. By focusing on the *types* of qualities that you want and the *types* of experiences that you want to have, your soulmate is naturally brought into your life and the soulmate energy in your love life will increase.

Practicing the principle of non-identification will help you to stay balanced and attuned to the way you want things to work out in your love life. Soulmate energy can be very intense and if you lose your balance it is possible that your hasty, thoughtless reactions can keep your soulmate away. This is not a punishment, but a fact of life. No relationship can "save" us from having to develop our relationship skills to the utmost.

The Spiritual Soulmate Vision

The exercise is a means of tapping into the higher, vibrating force of spiritual energy and connecting that force with your **Soulmate Process**. There are some props you can use, such as a candle, incense, New Age music, a favorite crystal, the drawing of the **Soulmate Symbol** in your Relationship Journal. Do not limit your application of this exercise by making it too elaborate. Use these props for special applications but also practice this exercise without them.

Exercise 7: The Spiritual Soulmate Vision

1. Light the candle and the incense. Play the music gently in the background. Hold the crystal in your left hand and the drawing of the Soulmate Symbol in your right. The "props" are to help you to achieve a mood of sacredness and love and to attune to soulmate energy.

2. Seat yourself comfortably.

3. Take three slow, gentle, full breaths and enter the state of *attention without tension.*

4. Look at the Soulmate Symbol you are holding. Take a long, slow breath as you imagine that you are drawing the experience of your soulmate relationship into your life with your breath.

5. State this affirmation: "I and my soulmate are together."

6. Close your eyes and imagine the Triangle of Soulmate Love surrounding you. Imagine it made of beautiful, shimmering light.

7. Now, imagine that you are sitting below one of the base angles. The triangle is now gigantic.

8. You look up and you see the giant flame of soulmate love and harmony alive, glowing, dancing in the center of the great triangle. You feel the divine love radiating from it.

9. You look down at your own chest and see a smaller version of that same flame dancing in your heart. You smile as you realize that the flame of divine love which nurtures all of us from the center of the universe is glowing in you.

10. You look along the base of the giant triangle to see who is seated at the other end. You expect to see your soulmate there, but the space is empty.

11. You look above to the apex of the triangle. It is also empty.

12. Once again state the affirmation, slowly and clearly, but this time imagine that you hear the voice of God stating it in you: "I and my soulmate are together."

13. Feel a presence now at the other two points of the triangle. Look at each point and see the same flames dancing there.

14. Gradually, the glow around the flame at the other end of the Triangle's base takes form. There, you see the qualities of your soulmate. You do not direct the shaping process. Simply witness it and realize that all you have ever desired in a mate is forming there.

15. You look up to the top of the giant triangle to express your gratitude. There, you see a great, loving being. It could be a guardian angel, but then it seems like two beings in one. Then you realize that it is the union of your Higher Self with that of your soulmate. It is yourselves, and at the same time, it is a higher being, an agent of God.

16. The Divine agent opens its arms and now you see that it is androgynous. From its open palms above each of your heads streams forth a spiritual energy. It pours onto your heads and flows through your beings. It is a clear golden-yellow light and it fills you with peace, security and love. Allow yourself to dwell in the energy of grace and the miraculous creation of the universe.

17. Once again you state the affirmation, but this time, you are completely aware that it is the single voice of all three of you: "I and my soulmate are together."

18. The forms of all three of you fade into the single giant flame burning within the great triangle. Now state aloud: "It is done" and know that it is being stated by the three voices in unison. Understand that this statement means you and your soulmate have established your connection on the inner planes of higher consciousness and now, the manifestation is destined.

19. Open your eyes gently and look about your room. Feel yourself back down to earth. Give yourself a minute to feel grounded.

20. Finally, feel a sacred kiss upon your lips—it is the kiss of your soulmate.

21. Rise to your feet when you are ready. Stand and stretch and know that it is done. The manifestation of your soulmate relationship has been determined to manifest by the most sacred, ruling force of the Universe.

Tarot Image 1: The Magician

We began this chapter with Tarot Image 1: *The Magician.* It symbolizes the power to direct your subconscious mind with your will. Above his head is a figure eight lying on its side, the mathematical symbol for infinity. It represents the seed of the infinite which is in each one of us, and which contains the seed-pattern of our growth along the lines of Cosmic Will.

The Magician's right hand is held high. In it he grasps a vertical wand, an ancient symbol of authority, power and will. The upraised wand symbolizes that the Magician's Will is raised above personal desires to control, and is offered up to be an instrument of the Higher Will that rules the Cosmos.

His left hand is pointing down to the earth. This pose makes him appear to be a channel through which Cosmic Will streams to do its work upon the earth. In fact, that is exactly what this image represents: the unity of individual will with Cosmic Will, which is the aim of our work upon trust.

By meditating on this image, your personal will is subconsciously aligned with the Cosmic Will, and you become the magician, a cosmic co-creator in the garden of your destiny. It also develops your abilities to concentrate, to see through appearances, to understand inner meaning, to recognize what you are focusing on, and to direct the focus of your attention at will.

Try this meditation on The Magician now, and notice the inner peace, the sense of focus and clarity, and the sense of being at one with Cosmic Will that it brings.

Exercise 8: The Magician

1. Take three slow, gentle, full breaths.

2. Meditate on Tarot card 1 for one to three minutes. Simply look at the details of the picture and imagine that the image is entering you through your attention. Feel the image impressing itself on the core of your being. Know that the picture is teaching you how to utilize your will and attention to actualize your limitless potential and fulfill your life purpose.

3. State this affirmation slowly and clearly three times: "My attention and will are perfectly aligned with Spiritual or Cosmic Will." As you state this, be open to receiving the meaning of the words.

CHAPTER

Tarot Image 2: The High Priestess

4

Maintain Your Balance

We can understand a soulmate relationship to be the highest potential of an intimate, loving relationship. Such a relationship is only possible to the extent that the lovers are expressing their highest potential as individuals. The more intelligently and skillfully we apply our own creative forces in our relationships, the better our relationship experiences will be.

Your words, thoughts, feelings and actions will affect your relationships, or your experience of being without one. As these are applied consciously, you can see the effects that they are having and respond accordingly. In this way, you grow in wisdom, in power and in love, and your love life will reflect your growth back to you.

Every relationship will go up and down. Nothing in nature can maintain its highest level. If you believe that your relationship is different, that yours is going to maintain its peak of harmonious bliss, take a good look at your inner self. State the following affirmation three times, slowly and clearly, as you observe your inner feelings: "I am completely open and honest with myself regarding my innermost feelings." Intuitively, we all know the truth.

This affirmation is a helpful way of awakening us to our deeper intuitive sense. Try it right now. If done on a regular basis, the affirmation, combined with the focus on feelings, can help you toward a higher state of consciousness in all matters.

Maintaining balance during the high cycles of a romantic

relationship can be difficult. We want to abandon ourselves to the passion of love. We want to believe that we have finally found our savior, our source and our release from life's pressures. However, losing yourself when all seems wonderful virtually guarantees that you will over-react when difficulties, setbacks and disappointments arise.

Maintaining balance in a low cycle builds strength and skill in handling the high cycles. In balance, you can receive your higher, inner, guiding light that will show you what to do for the good of your love life. If you are in a relationship, it will show you how you can build lasting richness into your union. You set up resistance to the high cycles to the same extent that you are unbalanced in the low cycles, thus making it difficult to seize your opportunities for bringing lasting improvement into your love life.

There is a way to make any experience work for you, a way to help your fellow human beings and solve even the most alarming global problems. That way is out there, waiting only for you to imagine it. And your imagination will obey your clear command.

Whatever your problem, gently, clearly and firmly inform your imagination, your subconscious, your inner self—or whatever else you want to call it—to come up with the solution. Direct it to show you the next step, or what to do to bring about what you want. Then, wait patiently and remain alert for the imaginative view or knowing of what you should do.

If you do not receive your answer today, ask again. Impatience, frustration and negative thinking will only make the wait more difficult. All this does is build an imaginary view of a hostile universe to which you will react as if it were true.

Resist the temptation to imagine the worst even when it seems that defeat stands at your doorstep. Direct your imagination to show you how to improve things. It will obey your command.

Defeat is just a point of view that in itself is self-defeating. Even if you seem to be defeated in one way, you can use your imagination to show you how to turn that defeat into a triumph equal to or greater than whatever you have lost.

You can direct your imagination in **The Soulmate Process** with a simple verbal command. The more calm, peaceful and centered you are when you do this, the more effective it seems to be. Bring to mind your current relationship situation or problem that you want guidance in, and then state: "Show me the wise way to proceed in this situation." Await your answer patiently, alert to recognize its arrival. Take a nap or go on about your business. It may come instantly or it may take days.

Thomas Edison used this approach to find his way through difficult stages in the invention process. He would clarify the problem he was facing and then take a nap, confident that he would awaken with the answer. He did.

It has been said that the most powerful act of our entire day is the last thought we have before going to sleep at night. This is because the thought impresses the deepest part of the subconscious and directs our creative forces to work in that direction.

Each evening, let one of your last thoughts be a request for guidance, or a clear focus on a situation in which you want guidance. First thing in the morning, recall the question you asked or the problem you were working on and check to see if there has been any progress.

The Future's Past Love life

If you were currently in a fulfilling, soulmate relationship, it would change your view of your entire life. Looking back on your life you would see each experience as a step along the way leading to this point. Every past event was preparing you for the joy of fulfillment you are currently experiencing.

Imagine now that you are looking back at your present life from that vantage point. See what you are going through as a stage in your fulfilling love story.

Use this affirmation to assist you, stating it three times, slowly and clearly: "My current experience is a stage in my journey to fulfilling love." As you state it, focus on the inner feeling of its reality. Do this exercise for as long as you like. Practice it regularly. The more you use it, the more powerful your experience of it will be.

This exercise builds trust and confidence that you will have the relationship that you want. It has a tendency to turn sorrow into joy. It also directs energy into the manifestation of the relationship you desire.

The Tree of Life

Kabbalah portrays the importance of the union of male and female energies as illustrated on the **Tree of Life** diagram on page 9. Take a look at the diagram now. Notice the three columns of spheres on the Tree. These columns are called the **Three Pillars**. The right-hand Pillar (spheres 2, 4 and 7) represents male, active or outflowing force. The left-hand Pillar (spheres 3, 5 and 8) represent female, receptive or inflowing force. The middle Pillar (spheres 1, 6, 9 and 10) represents the balanced union between opposites.

This diagram represents the polarized universe, created and sustained by the balanced union of male and female energy. Kabbalah has a saying: "As in the greater, so in the lesser; as above, so below; as within, so without." This implies that this principle of polarized union is not only at work in the universe at large, but also within each of us and in every aspect of our lives.

Our experiences teach us to develop balance. It is necessary, for example, to be assertive enough to express our true selves; this is a positive force expression. But it is also necessary to be trusting, receptive and flexible enough to allow others the same freedom; this expresses negative force. When we are balanced in this way, it is possible that our relationships will demonstrate harmony.

The middle Pillar on **The Tree of Life** represents the binding

force of the universe, the dynamic tension betwer
yang. Balance binds, imbalance pulls apart. For exain,
certain degree of aggression is needed to achieve our goals.
However, if we become too aggressive, we will over-react to not
having our way and that can be very destructive.

In addition to representing the principle of balance, the **Tree
of Life** diagram symbolizes the spiritual growth process, as well
as the ten essential cosmic forces which rule our lives. Your life
in naturally headed toward harmony and peace and spiritual
enlightenment. In fact, it is already there, you just need to
awaken to it. Thinking, feeling and acting as if we need to take
personal control in order to get what we do not have only
compounds our difficulties and makes us feel empty, lost and
alone. To the extent that you align your forces with Cosmic Will,
greater beauty, harmony and balance will unfold naturally in
every area of your life.

The lowest Sphere on the Tree is named **Kingdom**. It represents the physical level. That is where your consciousness is
focused when you look at the pages of this book. The Kingdom
represents awareness of the physical level.

The ninth Sphere on the Tree is named **Foundation**. Among
other things, it represents our unconscious motivations. The
real spiritual journey begins when we direct our attention
inward in order to uncover our motivations. Until then, one
may think that one is aligning with the Cosmic Will, when in
fact it is the personal ego running the show. The foundation also
represents the fact that Cosmic Will is the eternally strong
support of our existence.

The eighth Sphere is named **Honor**. Among other things, it
represents the intellect. As I said earlier, until I actually began
working on being aware of my thinking, I had no idea how
automatic, inefficient and self-defeating my thinking was. As
we become more aware of our inner selves and observe what
is motivating us, it then becomes our task to place the power of
our intellect under the direction of the Cosmic Will. Every time

your thinking is run by mindless habit, emotion or desire, it is under the control of the personal ego. Honor also represents the fact that everything the Cosmic Will does is eternally sacred.

The seventh Sphere is named **Victory**. It represents the power of emotion and desire. To the extent that you identify with your emotional reactions and are run by personal desires, you are resistant to the Cosmic Will. There is nothing intrinsically wrong with emotion and desire, but as with the intellect, our task is to place them at the disposal of Higher Consciousness. Victory also represents the fact that Cosmic Will is eternally victorious and can never be overcome by personal ego.

The sixth Sphere on the Tree is named **Beauty**. It represents the spiritual sun which shines the light of true individuality into our lives. The Cosmos has a plan for you. Sphere six receives it from above and then illumines the path for you that is aligned with it. This path remains hidden as long as one is obsessed with taking personal control of his or her own life. We must then come back lifetime after lifetime and go through the suffering and pain of being run by the personal ego until we are ready to trust the Cosmic Will. Beauty also represents the fact that the Cosmic Will is an expression of Divine Love.

Sphere five is named **Severity**. It represents the Cosmic elimination process. Loss occurs on all levels of this process. There is no escape from it. Just as we breathe out after breathing in, a cycle of loss, elimination and reduction occurs after a cycle of building, joining and expansion. Through loss, our path is made more straight in life and we are guided toward reliance on that which is eternal. Severity is also named **Justice**, representing the fact that Justice does rule the universe, even though it is not always trusted.

The fourth Sphere is named **Mercy**. It represents the opposite of severity. It symbolizes the process of building and expansion that is always going on. Look at your life and you will see that there is always something building, increasing, expanding. Even in times of most severe loss, something is expanding. The individual or True Ego resides in this Sphere. Its placement on the Tree symbolizes that all the Spheres below it are to be used by it. For instance, eventually, one reaches the level of awareness where the Cosmos no longer has to take anything away from him or her because he or she knows what must be given up and freely gives it. Mercy also represents the fact that Cosmic Will does demonstrate perfect mercy and grants us the abundance that we have proved we are ready to handle.

Sphere three is named **Understanding**. It represents the forces of restriction, containment and limitation. At each level of progress, one experiences some degree of limitation or containment. The personal ego generally despises limitation, however. This Sphere is also known as The Great Mother because the limitations which contain you are like a womb. You are protected and nurtured by what you cannot have, just as you are protected and nurtured by what you have. Freedom and restraint are equally necessary for the next step in true development. Understanding also represents the fact that Cosmic Will functions with perfect understanding far superior to what can be explained by the intellect.

Sphere two is named **Wisdom**. It represents the activity in the universe and in ourselves which stimulates growth, change and movement in line with Cosmic Will. It is this activity, being restrained by understanding, which gives birth to the universe. If there is too much activity, destruction and chaos ensue; that is why the restraints of understanding are important. Wisdom also represents the fact that the activity of Cosmic Will is perfectly wise.

Finally, we come to the highest Sphere on the Tree, the **Crown**. It represents the Cosmic Will which causes and rules Creation. It represents the greatest power in existence, the highest level of Divine Energy. The entire spiritual journey is aimed at reuniting with this point. However, we do not even begin work on that return until we have become fully established in Sphere four, where our true individuality resides.

Meditating on the Tree of Life diagram and what it represents subtly awakens consciousness on the inner levels of self, and reminds us of the real spiritual process we are in. The Tree as a whole represents the Self that is in perfect balance and alignment with Cosmic Will on every level. The physical conditions (Sphere 10) and the forces of the personal ego (Spheres 9, 8 and 7), are guided by the True Light (Sphere 6) of the individual ego or Higher Self (Sphere 4).

As you become more familiar with this diagram, you can use it to help you recognize when your personal ego is in control. The most common way the personal ego interferes with true spiritual process is represented by the pathways connecting Spheres seven, eight, nine and ten. When we have an idea or thought (Sphere 8) and connect it with a strong desire or emotional charge (Sphere 7), it goes into our unconscious as a belief program; we then act on the physical level (Sphere 10) as if what we believe is true. Our work as spiritual beings is to direct our attention inward in order to make this inner process conscious. When we are aware of the activities of the personal ego, we can stop identifying with them. This permits the harmonizing, balancing forces to do their work more freely.

Exercise 9: The Tree of Life

1. Take three slow, gentle, full breaths and gently enter the state of focused relaxation known as *attention without tension*.

2. Look at the Tree of Life diagram for the next three minutes. As you inhale, imagine the pattern of its Paths and Spheres entering your innermost being, stimulating your cells into balanced, harmonious vibration and aligning your physical, emotional, desire and intellectual forces with your highest, spiritual urge.

3. At the end of three minutes, state the following affirmation: "As I am the Tree and the Tree is me, the forces of the universe are aligned in me." Repeat this three times to help you deeply feel the meaning the words represent.

Fruit of Imbalance

When I was sixteen my girlfriend went away to college. We had been going together off and on (mostly on) since we were twelve. We were best friends as well as lovers. We did everything together.

When she left, I was crushed. I walked around in a deep blue funk. I thought this was romantic, the way someone in love was supposed to be, so I allowed myself to wallow in it. I didn't eat. I couldn't work. We ran up an enormous phone bill. In today's vernacular I probably would have been labelled a relationship addict.

Eventually, however, I was destined to realize the harm in my emotional dependency.

Years later, while my first marriage was in the process of breaking up, my emotions were more out of control than ever before. As a result of this emotional turmoil, I could not keep my mind on my work and it steadily suffered until my career hit bottom. I found myself obsessed with a woman that I did not even know if I truly loved. I was unable to apply all that I had learned about life, wisdom and the spiritual path. I went broke, had an identity crisis, and felt the shadow of madness looming over me as I strained under the pressure of constant anxiety.

I didn't understand what was causing this destructive cycle. It was only upon looking back that I realized I had merely been reaping the fruits of the seeds of imbalance I had planted back when my high school sweetheart went off to college. My patterns of emotional dependency had been lying in wait for me, ready for the right combination of circumstances to explode into their most destructive fury.

I am grateful for what I went through. I learned something important about life firsthand. I learned through experience that when I am out of balance emotionally, my reactions only create a bigger mess of my life.

Imagining Balance

Maintaining your balance does not have to take all the joy out of life. It simply gives you the ability to make better choices based on clearer thinking, more accurate observation, and the higher guiding light of your intuition.

The balanced state releases your power to direct your own life along the lines of your deepest, most inspiring vision. When you can register what is happening from a balanced point, you can tune into your own highest life wisdom to guide you. You can listen to your heart and hear its compassionate counsel. You can direct your imagination to show you what you truly want to happen and what you can do to bring it about.

When we are out of balance, our imagination is out of our control and we react to what is presented to us. Our expectations are out of line with reality, and we project them unrealistically.

A common misperception that blocks seeking a balanced state is the fear that if we find peace with conditions as they are, we will lack the motivation to improve things. This seems logical, and yet the exact opposite is the truth.

You will attract to you the conditions that you focus on within. The more vivid, deep and precise your imaginary vision and feelings of the experience you want, the more harmonious the reality will be. The balanced state is the foundation for directing your inner tuning and following your own highest guidance to your goals.

One of the ways to develop your ability to live in balance is to intentionally remember the balanced state. This memory of balance will draw it to you—your subconscious will get the message that this is what you want and give it to you. Remembering the balanced state may not result in drastic, immediate improvements, but gradually, the seed of your intention will become the fruit of your expression and eventually it will become a habit. Your ability to stay attuned to the way you want things to be and to follow your own highest guidance to your goals will steadily strengthen, deepen and grow.

Walk Through The Desert

When Rob told her that he was interested in someone else, Phyllis felt like her entire world had collapsed. She had never experienced such a loss of emotional and physical control. She began hyperventilating and sobbing as waves of panic raced through her. She dropped the phone and walked outside.

Phyllis knew that she needed to regain her self-control. She began focusing on her breathing as she headed down the street. She turned into the desert preserve that was behind her apartment complex. It was evening, but Phoenix in September is toasty warm all night.

She held her attention on her breathing. She observed the feeling of the air moving in and out through her nose or mouth. Every time her mind drifted back to the phone call, to images of Rob or of the other woman (whom she had never seen, but whom she imagined to be blonder, more passionate and more voluptuous than herself), emotional agony swept through her.

She focused on her breathing. Every time a negative thought surfaced, she refocused on her breathing in the now. She noticed that each time she focused on her breathing, the painful feelings and nightmare images of betrayal and humiliation vanished. They stayed away as long as she remained focused on the physical sensations of breathing.

For a while, the images played tug-of-war with her mind. Her thoughts would turn on, she focused on her breath. A thought would once again grab hold of her attention, and once more she would drop it and refocus on her breath.

Subtly, she began to win the war. As she continued her walk through the moonlit desert preserve, she began slowly to relax. Soon, she noticed the pleasant smell of desert sage.

How nice, she found herself thinking, to be able to walk like this at night. She remembered how cold it used to be in Michigan, where she grew up. *Breathing, breathing, focus on breathing,* she told herself.

The Saguaro cactus looked beautiful in the moonlight, like friendly giants watching over her. *Breathing, breathing, focus on breathing.*

She inhaled deeply. She relaxed. Her focus on her breathing had won.

Until that moment, she had viewed herself as a victim of her emotions. Whenever a relationship ended in the past, she became deeply depressed and frequently experienced panic attacks. She had worked hard over the past year to develop control of her attention, so that she did not have to focus on the thoughts that sent her out of emotional balance.

And now she had won. The tension had left her and she felt breaking up with Rob was worth it if this was the reward. She did not bother to call him back when she entered her apartment. "Let him go if that is what he wants, but I am not going to wait around and be the loyal girlfriend while he explores a possible romance with someone else."

Rob called her two weeks later. She remained confident and kept her composure. He apologized, said he was in love with her, and asked her to marry him. She looked within to see how she felt. In the past, her fear of rejection would have forced her to accept. She looked at that fear now as a passing wave. Fear is not the basis for a marriage, she realized. How did she *really* feel about Rob?

"No," she said. "But thank you anyway."

Rob pursued Phyllis for several weeks, but got nowhere. Finally, he got the message and stopped calling. Phyllis spent the next year enjoying her feeling of emotional balance and independence. She didn't meet anyone interesting during that year, but she enjoyed herself and the emotional balance that supported her.

She met William at a friend's Fourth of July party. They discovered that they had very similar goals in life. They were destined to achieve many of them together.

Not Thinking

I have learned that a large part of the suffering involved in physical pain is caused by my imagination. Whenever I am in pain, I imagine that it will last forever. Adding to the suffering is my constant mental replay of the injury that occurred, which creates stress. I project possibilities that will make the pain worse or result in even more damage and create even more stress. And stress heightens the pain, perpetuating the cycle of pain, negative thinking and stress.

The ability to not think at will is a great help during periods of physical or emotional pressure, danger or pain. When I focus on the present and keep myself from thinking, any "problem" I have ceases to exist. I am where I am and naturally enter peace. What we view as problems is really just a way of thinking about a situation. Often, by not interfering with worry or fear, and by trusting our natural inclinations, nature guides our circumstances into peace, balance and harmony in the same way water seeks a still state, naturally coming to a rest whenever outside agencies stop stirring it into a turbulent state.

The following exercise strengthens awareness and the ability to control and direct attention for achieving and maintaining emotional balance. It also results in a deepening and awakening of consciousness for more enlightened living. It is based on the ancient Buddhist practice of *mindfulness*, and is thousands of years old.

Do this exercise for as long as you like. A minimum of three to five minutes is usually necessary to experience any change, but any amount of time is better than none. I have done this for as long as forty-five minutes at a time and the results were glorious. I felt completely free of having to think, emote or desire. I experienced a quality of luminous reality that was more pure, more *real*, and more direct than I had ever known. These experiences remain vivid and clear in my memory nearly twenty years later.

This exercise not only strengthens and clarifies awareness, it develops your ability to *not-think* at will. After practicing it regularly for some time, you will find that you can stop thinking along any useless, undesirable line of thought you choose by simply focusing your attention on your breathing in the present.

I cannot recommend this exercise too highly. It is taught in Buddhism that it is the road to liberation from suffering. Practice it daily for one month if you want to see dramatic improvements in your life. You can practice it in bed in the evening before going to sleep.

Exercise 10: Conscious Breathing

1. You can do this exercise seated, standing, or even walking. If seated, get comfortable, and spine erect. Place your feet flat on the floor or cross your legs.

2. Close your eyes and focus your attention on your breathing. Observe the air as it flows in and out through your nose (or mouth if breathing through the nose is a problem).

3. As the air is flowing in, notice the physical sensations caused by it flowing in.

4. When the breath has reached its peak, observe the physical sensations when no air is flowing.

5. When you are exhaling, observe the physical sensations of the air flowing outward.

6. When your exhalation has reached its peak, observe the physical sensations when no air is flowing.

7. When you are inhaling, be aware that you are inhaling.

8. When you are exhaling, be aware that you are exhaling.

9. Be aware when your inhalation has reached its peak.

10. Be aware when your exhalation has reached its peak.

11. Do not control your breathing. Observe your breathing as it flows naturally, controlled by the body, not your will.

12. Each time a thought of any kind enters, drop the thought instantly and redirect your focus to your breathing.

Waves of Love

Lois and her younger sister Anne sat on the beach, watching and listening to the waves and crashing surf. Anne was going through a rough time in her relationship. She found herself continually criticizing her lover. It seemed that he was incapable of doing things the way she liked them done, the way she admired.

"I tried the exercise you recommended," she said. "You know, the one where I watch my thinking and feeling. Well, I find that I'm thinking negatively about him a lot, thinking of him as inadequate. Then I find myself feeling low self-esteem, like what's wrong with me that I cannot be with someone who knows how to act."

"Do you still love him?"

"That's just it. I get so annoyed that I really don't know how I feel. He presses my anger buttons, that's for sure."

"But do you *love* him, Anne?"

"He can be so wonderful at times, but things are always in turmoil." She wrapped her arms protectively around her knees.

Lois spoke about cycles. "Everything goes up and down, like the ocean waves, " she said. "I found in my relationship with Rick that by accepting and understanding the inevitability of cycles, things stay more balanced and harmonious.

"This helps me to avoid taking it personally when he doesn't do what I want him to do. I understand that if it's not this, it'll be something else. No one can come through for me at all times. It's not a reflection on my worth as a human being or theirs, it's just the way life is."

"That sounds pretty depressing," Anne muttered, her voice muffled by the crashing surf.

"I used to feel that way too, until I began to realize it was just my reaction to the way things are. You can't change the laws of nature, but you can learn to adapt to them."

Anne watched a gull drop from the gray sky, plunge into the

ocean, and emerge with a fish. "As evolving human beings, we learned how to adapt physically to just about every condition on earth," she said thoughtfully, as much to herself as to her companion. "I guess it makes sense that we have to learn how to adapt to the laws of life emotionally as well." A flock of squawking gulls filled the sky with their laughter. She unwrapped her arms from around her knees, straightened out her legs and placed her hand around her sister's. "Thanks, Sis."

The Law of Cycles

One of the laws in the natural order of life is the Law of Cyclic Alternation. Everything in nature follows an alternating, cyclic pattern. Winter alternates with summer, spring with autumn. These seasons also occur in our love lives.

By imagining that we live in a universe that is *not* characterized by cycles, we guarantee unnecessary suffering based on misevaluation. Positive and negative cycles will always alternate. Therefore, it is wise to learn how to accept and live in *both*. As you progress in your ability to do this, you will find your experiences of both cycles gaining in richness, joy and meaning.

One way I have caused myself needless suffering is by formulating opinions about myself, my life, other people, the world, while in an unbalanced state. When I feel good, I see only what I want to see and overlook important details. This leads to disappointment. When I judge from a low, angry or unhappy state, everything seems hopeless and I overlook opportunities.

The way I respond in a low cycle affects how I respond in my next high cycle. The more balanced I can remain when things are not going the way I want them to go, the more balanced I can remain when things are going well. The reverse is also true.

There is a way to become more clearly aware of your present internal state and how to deal with it. I call it the *Relationship Wave*. In your Relationship Journal, draw a wave. At the highest point, mark a plus sign, at the lowest, a minus sign. This represents the recurring cycles in all things. Where on this cycle would you presently chart your love life? If it is completely satisfying, place it at the highest point of the wave. If it seems . the worst it has ever been, place it at the bottom of the wave.

Look at the wave you drew and notice that in addition to the high point and the low point, there are also three midpoints. Number these midpoints one, two and three. If your current position seems to be in the middle, not so hot but nothing to grieve over, place yourself at one of the midpoints. It does not matter which outer midpoint you choose (#1 or #3) since both predict the same future and have the same past. However, choose the midpoint #2 if your previous cycle was a high cycle compared with where you are right now.

The nearer you are to what feels like a balanced, harmonious internal state, the closer to one of the numbered midpoints you should place yourself. To the extent you feel enthused and excited, place yourself higher on the wave. To the extent you feel low in mood, health or vitality, position yourself lower on the wave.

This exercise helps me to measure the distance between my present state and the state of balance. This is important to me because I know that to the degree that I am out of balance, either high or low, I must be extra careful in my thoughts, feelings, speech and actions. It is easy to deepen and empower a state of imbalance with hasty reactions. Frequently, when I record my current state on the wave, I am pleased to realize that I am not as unbalanced as I may have thought I was.

As you keep your *Relationship Wave* chart, you will eventually discover for yourself the wave-like pattern of events. By remembering during low cycles that high cycles are bound to follow, you will be inspired with realistic hope. By remembering, during peak times that conditions cannot maintain at that high level, you will be less disappointed, frightened or confused when the inevitable low cycles follow.

Use this affirmation to bring about a more balanced, harmonious state: "My state is balanced in perfect harmony and peace." State this affirmation three times; each time, focus your attention on the experience which the words represent.

Tarot Image 2: *The High Priestess*

We began this chapter with Tarot Image 2: *The High Priestess*. This image symbolizes the function of the subconscious mind, which is the pure, receptive channel of higher consciousness. The veil behind her symbolizes that she is your access to hidden knowledge. When she is approached in the correct way, which begins with inner peace and poise, the veil is lifted and the knowledge you seek will be revealed.

Her position, seated between a black and white pillar, signifies balance, poise and equanimity. This is also represented by the equal-armed cross on her gown. The elaborate lunar head-dress indicates that she represents the subconscious mind—the moon is an ancient symbol of the subconscious, which projects the images and ideas of reality that the ignorant believe to be real and caused by outside forces beyond their control. The enlightened understand the subconscious can be lovingly directed by their higher will, wisdom and love.

Exercise 11: The High Priestess

1. Take three slow, gentle, full breaths.
2. Meditate on Tarot Image 2 for one to three minutes. Simply look at the details of the picture and imagine that the image is entering you through your attention. Feel the image impressing itself on the core of your being. Imagine the picture is teaching you how to use the powers of your subconscious to actualize your limitless potential and fulfill your life purpose.
3. State the following affirmation: "My subconscious is wholly aligned with the fulfillment of my spiritual potential."
4. Having stated this affirmation, know that the High Priestess within you is aligning with Higher Mind to manifest the experiences best for you.

CHAPTER ━━━━━━━━

Tarot Image 3: The Empress

5

Trust and Worthiness

It has been written that when the bottom drops out it becomes the top. Ninety-nine percent of our suffering comes from a lack of trust. Lacking trust we resist change because we perceive it as loss. And yet, it is only the loss of our previous limitations; we struggle against growing beyond those previous limitations, into greater power, liberation and joy.

George was approaching fifty when his wife left him for another man. Just when he thought that things could not get any worse, their only child, a seventeen-year-old son, was killed in an auto crash. He found himself feeling completely alone in the world, with no family, no close friends, and apparently no purpose.

His days consisted of working at a job that had no meaning for him. At the end of the day he would come home to his empty apartment with nothing else to do but wait for sleep to bring him release from his constant strain. In his journal, which he kept sporadically, he wrote that the most difficult thing for him was just keeping on.

When he charted his life on the wave-cyclic graph, he placed it at the bottom. As soon as he did this, he found himself feeling relieved. He began to understand that things would eventually have to get better. He also found himself feeling self-respect because of the extreme adversities he had endured.

But then it occurred to him that he might not be at the bottom of the wave. If someone had asked him years ago, even before he lost his son, he probably would have felt he was at the bottom then, and look at how much worse things had gotten! When this thought occurred to him his spirits took a nose-dive. But then, they surged again.

He suddenly felt completely fearless. There was nothing left to lose. He felt free. It no longer mattered if he was at the bottom, at the top or somewhere in-between. It had all become one. This feeling of complete liberation was the greatest experience of his life. As far as he was concerned it was more than worth all of the pain he had gone through.

Two weeks later, still feeling the high of his liberation, he saw an ad for volunteer tutors to teach troubled teens how to read. No teaching experience was required. All that was necessary is that applicants know how to read. He knew instantly that this job was for him.

The job required four weekly preparation sessions, and then he began. He fell in love with the work. Helping these kids gave him a great sense of satisfaction. As much as he gave to them, he felt that they gave him even more.

His greatest strength as a tutor was his endless patience. It translated into results with those that other tutors had given up on. He was able to transmit his patience to his pupils and by not losing faith in them they found the support they needed to keep faith in themselves. George soon had a reputation as the most effective and most requested tutor.

His results did not go unnoticed by the head of the department of the community college which presented the program. Without letting George know what he was up to, the department head did everything he could to have George hired as a paid, full-time tutor. After eight months of pleading his case before the superintendent, he finally succeeded. George was offered the position at a salary that equaled what he was making at his full-time job with even better benefits. He was thrilled and accepted the job.

A couple of years passed. He was feeling such peace and purpose in his new life that he could not imagine things improving. His relationship with his pupils was more than professional. He loved every one of them and stayed in contact with a good number of them through written correspondence.

One day, the mother of one of his pupils came to see him. Her son was not only reading, but his discipline problems had vanished. His new friends were not gang members like the old ones had been. She had to meet this man and thank him for helping to turn her son's life around.

She was a single mother. It was love at first sight. They were married six months later.

When George reflected upon his experiences, he came to understand that he had gained much through his losses. Enduring them gave him inner strength and patience, just as coming out of them instilled in him an unshakable trust in life.

He believed this inner strength, trust, and patience radiated from him like an aura, which attuned his pupils to their own. That is why he could take no credit for their achievement, although he was proud and grateful to be a part of it. He was convinced that it was *their own* inner strength, trust and patience which enabled them to learn to read and, more importantly, to believe in themselves.

He smiled as he thought of the fact that his son's death did have meaning after all. And he laughed when he realized that he was grateful to his ex-wife for leaving, and to her lover who had taken her away, and for all the good things that had happened which were rooted in his darkness and his pain.

Balance of Trust

On a clean page in your Relationship Journal, draw another equilateral triangle. Label the top point "Balance." Label the left angle "Acceptance" with a minus sign beneath it. Label the right angle "Direction" with a plus sign beneath it. Above the word "Balance," draw a figure eight laying on its side. Inside the triangle, draw a circle and put a black dot in the center of the circle. This triangle represents the balance of trust. When we focus on our dreams of what we want, it is important to remember to remain unattached to our visions of the future so that we don't become unhappy, dissatisfied, and out of balance with the way things are.

The vision of the love life you want is like a seed you have planted. Every time you focus on that seed from a balanced state, you nurture its growth into the events of your destiny. However, Universal Law rules the timing of this process, just as it rules the growth of plants and all other living things.

The minus sign beneath the left angle represents a receptive condition. This refers to your ability to accept and enjoy whatever is happening, to trust that a higher purpose is being served even when you do not know what that purpose is.

The plus sign beneath the right angle represents an active, out-flowing influence. This refers to your efforts to direct your life toward the vision of love that you cultivate and focus upon within.

If there is imbalance between these two forces, we block **The Soulmate Process**. Too much focus on direction can make us impatient and frustrated so we overreact when things do not happen the way we want them to happen or as quickly as we want. Too much acceptance and we act like victims who believe they are at the mercy of the fates, or who strive to win the acceptance and approval of others to whom we have given our power.

The mathematical symbol for infinity (the figure eight on its side) represents the freedom to be at peace in the now that we experience when we balance acceptance and direction.

The circle with a dot at its center is an ancient symbol of the balanced, centered state, and the true self expression which naturally flows from it. We can use this symbol as a device to center and attune our beings to our innermost self, the eternal spiritual being we truly are and the spiritual process or spiritual purpose which is ours to fulfill.

The Soulmate Process works best when applied with the

Balance of Trust. The *Balance of Trust* means that you trust enough in what is happening to be at peace with the way things are, and that you trust enough in what is possible to focus on your goals and pursue them.

Be alert to notice when you are losing your *Balance of Trust.* If you are becoming impatient, frustrated, or depressed over the way things are, you are probably becoming too positive in the sense of being overly attached to your goals. If you are feeling powerless to change things, or find yourself being overly dependent or demanding of others, you are probably becoming too negative and overlooking your creative power to direct your own life.

One solution to imbalance is compensation. If you find yourself in victim consciousness, focus on your inner vision of the love life experiences you want. If you find yourself becoming overly attached to having things the way you envision or desire them, stop focusing on the future and remind yourself to relax, trust and enjoy yourself in the present. Your energy will follow the direction of your attention.

Use the Balance of Trust diagram to balance your power of acceptance and direction. Hold the point of a pen, pencil, or index finger on the central dot of the circle in the triangle. Imagine that this point is the energy of balance between your powers of acceptance and direction. Now imagine that this balancing power is streaming into you.

Imagine that the circle around the point is now surrounding you. It keeps out all unbalancing forces and tendencies. Within the circle is perfect balance and trust, concentrated into its essence at the central point.

Inhale slowly and imagine that you are inhaling the energy of balance and trust. Feel yourself opening to trust in your purpose and the possibility that the future you envision can and will happen. As you exhale, imagine that you are filling your very being with this pure power of balance and trust. Take three complete breaths with this focus.

When you feel ready to leave this delightful focus, clap one time and pause for a moment, then clap twice and pause for a moment, then clap three times. Following the third and final clap, state aloud: "It is done. Trust and balance are in me now."

Clapping, pointing your index finger and holding a staff-shaped object (such as a pen or pencil) are all ancient symbols of authority, will, and power. They suggest to your subconscious that you are directing it to receive the energy that you focus on. The first clap is for your positive power to direct. Two claps are for the negative power to accept. Three claps are for the balancing of the two, which opens you to infinity.

Accepting Love

Vanessa believed that as long as she was overweight, she would not find someone to love her. This led to feelings of self-pity, which turned into depression. When she was depressed, she overate and lacked the motivation to exercise.

When she was depressed, she was short-tempered and negative in her relationships with friends, clients and family members. Her depression made her feel isolated and lonely. Even if she met her potential soulmate, she believed, her body would turn him off and if that didn't, her attitude would.

One day she realized that the more she resisted her problems, the stronger they seemed to become. She tried another approach. Instead of condemning herself for her physical condition, she worked on cultivating the conviction that she was worthy of the loving relationship she wanted just the way she was. She cultivated this new feeling about herself by using this affirmation: "I am worthy of the loving relationship I want." As she stated this, she focused on the inner feeling and knowing which the words represented.

At first, she felt only resistance to this new way of seeing herself. But gradually, she began to feel better about herself. She began to see through her physical self as if it had become transparent and began to recognize her qualities that were admirable and attractive. Her attitude toward herself and her love life slowly changed. She allowed herself to be loved and soon she was dating. Then she was married to the kindest, most wonderful man she had ever known.

The Secret Wisdom of Romantic Fools

When we feel undeserving or unworthy of the relationship experience that we want, we are subtly keeping it away. I used to believe that the values I gave to things were caused by those things, and that I was helpless to change my feelings about them. If I wanted something, I thought that it was because there was something intrinsically valuable or desirable in what I wanted. If I disliked something or someone, I was convinced that it was because there was something intrinsic to that other person or thing that was undesirable. If I did not live up to my own expectations, I was not worthy of my own respect and love, let alone anyone else's.

Then I learned that we cultivate our values. It seems our "loves and hates" have less to do with reality than with the way we happen to look at it. Most of the time, this happens unconsciously. Often, we are influenced by another's values and interests.

You can cultivate your values and interests consciously and intentionally to bring out your higher potential and achieve your greatest dreams by focusing your attention on the desirable possibilities of an object. If you repeatedly imagine yourself experiencing pleasure when you eat chocolate cake, your craving for chocolate cake will strengthen. If you regularly imagine yourself enjoying the feeling of being slender and trim, your motivation to diet and exercise will be strengthened.

We have all done things in the past that we can interpret in a way that blocks us from happiness. We can see the way we hurt or disappointed others and decide we deserve to be hurt and disappointed in return. Or we can learn to forgive ourselves.

Forgiveness has more to do with moving on than it has to do

with looking back. As you cultivate your feeling of worthiness for what you want in life, you are forgiving yourself for failing to live up to your expectations in the past.

We can always view ourselves and what we have to offer as inferior, inadequate, unworthy. It has nothing to do with our actual selves or our performance. It is a matter of identifying with a particular way of looking at ourselves.

When you build within yourself the knowledge that you deserve a relationship experience, two very important things occur. First, you open yourself to receive that experience. Second, you actually attract that experience into your life.

Accepting that an intimate, loving relationship can be one of the most precious experiences in life will naturally elicit your romantic self-expression.

Exercise 12: Opening to Love and Romance

1. Take three slow, gentle, full breaths and quietly enter the state of focused relaxation known as *attention without tension.*

2. Close your eyes and imagine being with your soulmate, the loving partner of your innermost dreams. Focus on the feeling of your being together. Experience the joy. If you can, imagine the particular physical qualities of your soulmate, but do not identify them with anyone in particular. Focus on the *types* of qualities you find desirable in your soulmate and the harmonious way that you relate together.

3. State the following affirmation slowly and clearly, focusing on the reality which the words represent: "I am worthy of the soulmate experience which fulfills and satisfies my deepest dreams of love and it is aligned with my spiritual purpose and the expression of my highest potential on every level."

4. Continue to focus on this inner experience and to repeat the affirmation for as long as you like.

With practice, you will come to accept that you can have all the joy and fulfillment of the romantic relationship of your dreams while still fulfilling your individual goals and life purpose. You will see the joy of a satisfying love life as a natural extension of a life which fulfills its highest purpose, rather than as a distraction, obstruction or intrusion.

This deep, inner perception releases us to express our romantic natures freely and energetically, because it removes the fear that we are losing touch with more "practical" or "important" matters by doing so. It also frees us to receive, as well as draw out, the romantic expressions of others by cultivating our feelings of self-worth and freeing us from any blockages we might have that are rooted in a lack of self-forgiveness from the past.

Finally, practicing this exercise helps us to imagine the potentials of a loving, harmonious intimate relationship that we can cherish and adore. In other words, it naturally makes of us wisely romantic fools.

Healing Past Hurt

Each time Zackery tried to imagine the kind of relationship that he wanted, he felt it was useless. He'd already had the relationship he wanted; it ended when Lori left him. He could not think about happiness in a relationship without the fear of losing it instantly entering to crush his hopes.

As long as he believed he could not have the happiness of a loving relationship, he was unmotivated to make any effort in that direction. In fact, he found himself doing things that actually kept him out of a relationship. He stopped dating because he would plunge into a bad mood as soon as the date started. He found himself actually shying away from women, especially those he found attractive, run by the fear that he would only be hurt again in the end.

Eventually he came to realize his attitude was keeping him locked into the very reality he feared: a life without the joy of loving, intimate companionship. This disgusted him enough to work on turning things around. He knew he had to build his trust and confidence in the possibility of a joyous and fulfilling relationship. He used the following affirmation to help him to cultivate this trust: "I *can* have the loving, intimate, romantic relationship that fulfills me with deepest, lasting joy." As he stated this slowly and clearly, he focused on the lasting joy of love which the words represented.

He used this focus three times a day. Whenever he noticed the old patterns of avoiding intimacy, he focused on the reality he wanted. Gradually, he felt he was healing from his past hurt. As his trust strengthened, his attitude and motivation improved.

About a month after beginning this practice, he received a phone call from none other than Lori, the one who had left him a couple of years earlier. She said she thought of him often, she missed the fun they'd had together, she found herself thinking again and again over the last few weeks about how special he was, and how special their relationship had been.

During his exercise in developing trust he had always been careful not to focus on the relationship he'd had with Lori as the one that he wanted. Instead, he focused on the qualities of their relationship which he found desirable, but he never focused on the relationship itself. Her call amazed him.

Mathematics of Trust

Stated mathematically, your ability to manifest a satisfying love life is directly proportional to the extent you *trust* it can happen. Notice when you feel distrusting that the love you want can manifest. Practice feeling the state of trusting that your dream of a satisfying love life will come true. As you practice both of these, you liberate the power to make it happen.

The Power of Trust

Here is an exercise which not only builds trust, but also demonstrates its power to release you into joy and love.

Begin by imagining there is nothing between you and your perfect, unlimited joy and happiness. Imagine a happy, smiling, laughing infant and know it is you.

As you continue to imagine this lack of boundary between yourself and your utter joyfulness, state the following affirmation: "I am the power of my joy." As you state this, continue to focus on the experience of nothing between you and your joy.

When I have observed others practicing this exercise, I notice that they seem to find it impossible to keep from smiling.

When practiced diligently, this exercise results in a steady uplifting of my state. I enjoy practicing it when I am working. I simply remind myself again and again that there is nothing keeping me from joy, nothing standing in the way of my complete happiness here and now. By the end of a half hour or so of frequently reminding myself of this, I find it easier to laugh, my energy is higher, and my sense of humor seems recharged.

Now for the next stage of this exercise. Imagine there is nothing keeping you from experiencing total fulfillment in your love life. Imagine, trust, know, feel, accept that nothing is standing in your way—not time, not space, not circumstances—nothing.

Continue to imagine this, as you state the following affirmation: "I am the power of my completely fulfilling love life."

Repeat this affirmation again and again to help you to remain focused on imagining there is nothing between you and your complete satisfaction in a loving, intimate relationship. When done for five to ten minutes, the results can be amazing.

The practice of these two exercises builds trust in the certainty that we can be happy and fulfilled in life and in love. It demonstrates the power of trust as the barriers to joy and love seem to dissolve when the force of trust is intensified.

Tarot Image 3: The Empress

We began this chapter with Tarot Image 3: *The Empress*. This image represents fruitfulness and the activity of the creative imagination.

The water streaming past The Empress and down the waterfall represents the stream of consciousness springing from the subconscious mind that has received its direction through the conscious mind. We can presume that this water is responsible for the abundant growth which surrounds the seated woman. This portrays the creative power in the images we hold in mind and the imaginary experiences we focus on within: those images and imaginary experiences become the actual experiences we receive in our destiny.

Although the woman in the image is seated, this image symbolizes creative fertility and abundance of activity. It is traditionally presumed that she is pregnant. The great activity of the abundant scene is an outer representation of the internal activity of her pregnancy.

You are ripe with the imaginary experiences you focus upon. These gestate on the inner levels until they naturally emerge as the events of your life. What you conceive of within you will give birth to without.

Your imagination will respond with an infinite flow of imagination when you give it the direction of your intention. For example, if you want to experience more self-worth and the confidence that you can have the relationship you want, simply know your intention to recall or imagine those states. In time your subconscious must respond, filling your awareness with the experience.

The creative imagination is fertile and active in all of us but it must be directed to bear the best fruits. The Magician (Image 1) represents the focus of attention and intention with Higher, Divine, Cosmic or Spiritual Will. The High Priestess (Image 2) represents the receptive state of the subconscious, ready to receive the stimulus of The Magician which will activate the subconscious in line with Higher Will. The Empress (Image 3) represents the fruits of the activated subconscious and imagination: an abundance of creative images which generates the forms and patterns of our living experience in the most direct alignment with our spiritual growth.

To align your personal will with Cosmic Will and gain control of your attention, focus on Tarot Image 1. To deepen your receptivity and openness to suggestion from Higher Mind, focus on Tarot Image 2. To stimulate your creative imagination into action, focus on Tarot Image 3.

Exercise 13: The Empress

1. Take three slow, gentle, full breaths and enter the state of *attention without tension*.

2. Meditate on Tarot Image 3 for one to three minutes. Simply look at the details of the picture and imagine that the image is entering you through your attention. Feel the image impressing itself on the core of your being. Imagine that the picture is teaching you how to activate the flow of your creative imagination to enable you to reach your ultimate potential and fulfill your life purpose.

3. State the following affirmation slowly and clearly, with attention ready to recognize the reality which the words represent: "My creative imagination is aligned with Cosmic Will and manifesting the experiences which are best for me to have."

Know that The Empress within you is responding by giving birth to the experiences aligned with your greater spiritual potential.

CHAPTER

Tarot Image 4: The Emperor

6

Apply Purposeful Action

Sandy realized that her marriage was in serious trouble. Hanz, her husband, was so involved with his work there seemed to be no room for anything else in his life. She discussed her feelings with him and he promised he would change. He did change. He began spending even less time with her.

This did not merely go wrong for a week or a month. It continually worsened for a year and a half. The last time she brought up the issue, he became upset and responded by locking himself in the study where he worked till late in the evening. He slept on the couch that night for the first time in their marriage.

She met Lenny for the first time the following day. Lenny was very charming, and from the moment she saw him she was attracted. He gave her a look in the eye when they were introduced that literally sent chills up and down her spine.

While her problems with Hanz persisted, her relationship with Lenny progressed rapidly. They fell into deep and stimulating conversation nearly every time they passed one another. She never remembered exactly what they talked about but she *did* remember the way his eyes laughed knowingly whenever he looked at her.

Sometime later, Lenny invited her to lunch. They laughed so much she almost could not eat. At one point during the meal, Lenny interrupted her laughter when he took her hand and looked at her seriously. He touched her wedding ring and asked about her marriage.

It was against her better judgment to talk about her marital problems, especially to another man whom she found attractive. But she could not hold anything back when Lenny looked at her. "It's not good," she said.

"I knew it," he said. "Every time I think of you I feel this pain in my heart. I know you are unhappy. Look, if this guy is not treating you right, this might be the time to make your move. You won't be alone. I want you."

She drew her hand back and suddenly felt a huge wave of shame and doubt. For the first time she realized that she had been taking her husband's rejection personally. Her next thought was equally disturbing. As she looked at Lenny something that had never occurred to her suddenly seemed so obvious: Hanz was having an affair.

By the end of the day Sandy was completely exhausted. Her feelings for Lenny were only making things worse. The hurt and dissatisfaction she felt in her marriage left her feeling unsure of her real feelings for Lenny. And her strong attraction to Lenny, combined with the excitement over his interest in her, left her unsure of what to do about Hanz.

The only solution she could come up with was to become active instead of reactive. She stopped trying to get Hanz's attention, and she stopped worrying about missing her opportunity to be with Lenny. She focused instead on **The Soulmate Process**.

She began by making a list of what was "wrong" with her relationship with Hanz, and what was "right" with her relationship with Lenny. She disliked Hanz's disinterest, his withdrawal from intimacy, his failure to keep his promise to change. She loved Lenny's eyes, his attentiveness, and his ability to reach into her soul and bring out her secret self.

Then she listed what she liked about her marriage. She liked commitment and monogamy. She liked the stability of building a life together. And she still loved Hanz. He was handsome, charming and they had many wonderful memories, although this past year he had become so weary and emotionless. What she disliked about her relationship with Lenny was the lack of commitment, the betrayal of her vows by being with him romantically, and that she really did not know who he was and if their attraction was real.

She focused on the relationship that she wanted, without identifying it with either Hanz or Lenny. She practiced feeling worthy of it as well. She also remembered the principle of cycles. The cyclic perspective reminded her that perhaps these two relationships were merely at opposite ends of the wave right now. This could just be a low cycle in her marriage and a high cycle in her relationship with Lenny. This perspective helped her to remain more balanced and level-headed in her approach toward her attraction toward Lenny, and in her feelings of repulsion toward her husband. It helped her to detach and involve more of her power into constructive focus on her love life goals.

Sandy continued to practice regularly for weeks. She used the time that she was left alone to focus on the soulmate exercises. When she felt tempted to call Lenny, she applied a delay circuit during which she would practice focusing on the relationship she wanted for five minutes. At the end of this it always felt wrong to call him. She knew that to call him now would be a blind reaction to her loneliness that would only complicate matters. Sometimes she would practice the exercises for as much as two hours at a time. She began to enjoy these lengthier exercise periods. They strengthened her and she felt more secure within herself and more capable of making the best choices.

She emerged from each practice with the feeling of being in control of her own life. She lost her fear of losing her opportunity with Lenny. If he was her soulmate, then the relationship could not suffer from her balanced, self-honest approach. No relationship was worth being untrue to herself.

One evening, things finally became clear. Hanz was working

late and had missed dinner. Usually, he called to let her know. Now, he had not even done this. By the time she went to bed that evening, there was still no word from him and she believed she'd had enough.

The phone rang to wake her. It was the hospital. Hanz had been found by one of the cleaning-service workers, collapsed and unconscious.

When she arrived at the hospital the doctor reported that there was nothing medically wrong with Hanz. Apparently, he had just passed out from nervous exhaustion.

He was released and they went home. On the way, Hanz broke down and finally explained. "The business has been failing for a long time, Sandy. I invested too much into expansion. We've been on the verge of bankruptcy for the last year and a half."

She took his hand in hers as she continued driving. "But why haven't you told me anything? I could have shared your burden and made it lighter."

He began to cry. "I didn't feel worthy of your love. You are so wonderful. I guess I have been in love with you from the moment we met. But as long as I was failing in business I was too ashamed of myself. And I hoped that I could work everything out if I just worked long enough and hard enough."

Now she was crying with him. "I thought maybe there was someone else."

"Are you kidding? You're my soulmate." He took her hand and kissed it. "You know, when I was lying in the hospital room I thought for a moment that I was going to die. You know how crazy thoughts enter your mind. I figured I'd had a massive heart attack or something. But I didn't mind dying except for missing you. I love you so much, and I have missed you so much."

For a moment, she did not know how to respond. But an image of Lenny flashed in her mind. She saw him and heard him as clearly as if he were right there. "Go on, Sandy. Tell him you love him with all your heart. Tell him you'll stay with him as long as he never shuts you out again. Tell him if he will share his life with you, you will share your love with him."

"I never could hide anything from you, Lenny," she thought with a smile.

The Power of Action

There is power in actually doing things for what you want. We have five basic levels of action. These are represented by the five-pointed star we used in the alternate **Soulmate Chart** in Chapter Three. These levels are physical, emotional, mental, spiritual and social.

When all five levels are applied in balance toward a single goal we are utilizing our full potential of power. Let us now look at how to apply all five levels of action to achieve our love life goals.

1. Mental Level: One of the most important things we can do on this level is to clearly formulate our love life goals. By focusing on experiences we want to have, we awaken our own intuitive guidance.

The more intelligent, aware, knowledgable, compassionate and skillful we are, the better all of our life experiences will be. Mental self-development means increasing our knowledge, sharpening our thinking and communicating abilities, and developing the ability to concentrate or to direct attention.

Action: Take the next minute or two and do something on the mental level for your love life. This is really quite simple and easy because just thinking about what you can do to improve your love life is a mental act aimed at its improvement. Whether or not you arrive at an answer right away does not matter. Simply apply the act.

2. Physical Level: Physical level activity involves anything we do with our physical body. This level generally requires the most effort. It's generally easier to come up with the idea of giving someone flowers than it is to go to the store to buy them or to the garden to pick them. It's easier to say, "I love you," than it is to massage another's aching back at the end of a long, hard day.

Physical action aimed at improving your love life will depend upon your present love life circumstances. If you are not in a relationship, it might involve going to places where you have the opportunity of meeting someone, even if ninety-nine times out of a hundred nothing comes of it.

In our society it seems that many place too much importance on the physical level. All day long advertisers suggest to us that if we have white enough teeth, sleek enough cars, drink the right beer and wear the right gym shoes, all our romantic fantasies will come true. While it is true that the physical level is important, it is no substitute for the other levels. Overemphasizing the physical is no better than underemphasizing it.

The act of physical self-development includes doing things for health and fitness, developing the strengths and skills to adequately provide for yourself and those you are responsible for, to earn enough at a job or career you love in order to continue doing it, and to generally do things aimed at refining your physical self-expression.

Action: Stand and walk ten steps. As you make this physical effort, state the following affirmation again and again: "I am making this effort to set into motion a trend of physical action aimed at improving my love life." Any action done with a purpose will, in fact, set such an action trend into motion. The result is that you will find it easier to physically do things for what you want.

3. Emotional Level: Apply balance, direction and control on an emotional level. Feeling depressed, discouraged or frustrated only makes it more difficult to do what needs to be done and to endure what must be endured. Feeling inspired, expecting to succeed, and feeling confidence and self-esteem make it easier to do and accept what is necessary to achieve our goals.

The mental level rules the emotional, but all of the levels are connected. By focusing on what we want to experience we generally find ourselves growing more confident that we can achieve it. By persistently imagining the feelings of trust, confidence, self-esteem and motivation, we soon begin to feel them flowing through us.

Emotional self-development involves learning how to remain in emotional balance and harmony when you are receiving what you want and when you are not. You can actually utilize the most unpleasant experiences as opportunities to develop your ability to remain at peace, patient and trusting.

Action: Think back to a time you can recall becoming angry, upset, frustrated, impatient or depressed. Imagine yourself dealing with that situation from a more balanced state—secure, confident and at peace in the situation and handling it with skill, intelligence and love. This exercise actually transforms our emotional weakness and develops emotional strength.

4: Spiritual: The spiritual level has to do with your own sense of a Higher Power. Spiritual activities may include prayer, meditation, ritual, or disciplines. Taking time to attune yourself to the innermost core of Higher Power in your being is as important for your growth and well-being as food, water and air. Spiritual activities balance all your levels and align you with increased power and joy to live, to love, to understand and to create.

Spiritual self-development means heightening awareness of the eternal being, your True Self, which transcends the values, desires, likes and dislikes of your personal self. It means trusting and surrendering to the Power beyond your control and comprehension that is at work in your destiny. Spiritual development heightens your level of empowerment for higher functioning on all levels.

Action: Close your eyes and inhale slowly and deeply. Focus on the air streaming in and imagine that the air is the energy of God, your Higher Self, the Creative Core of the universe and all beings in it. When your lungs are full, state the following affirmation: "I and my spiritual being are One." As you state these words, imagine the pure spiritual energy filling the core of your being.

5. Social Level: The social level includes your interpersonal skills, such as communication, the ability to remain patient and tolerant when others do not do things your way, the strength and self-honesty to remain true to yourself, your awareness of your actions and reactions and the affects those have on others, etc. Obviously, your social skills will have an affect on your love life.

Social skills vary with different social settings. You would not relate with someone at work the way you would at a party. You would not relate with a child the way you would with an adult. You would not relate with a thief the way you would with someone who was offering you assistance. The ability to discern who you are dealing with and the setting of your relationship is essentially the ability to select your friends and associates and to treat people fairly.

Action: In the following section, you will learn an exercise for applying and developing the social skill of conscious relating for improving all of your relationships, including your most intimate one.

When applying the power of action, there are two important points to bear in mind. First is the principle of *non-attachment to results*. To be detached means that, although your actions have a purpose, you are not counting on a particular result.

Applying action for what you want will sooner or later bring you what you acted for. However, do not make your expectations overly specific. For instance, you may do something to improve your love life like going to a dance. It is quite possible that you will have absolutely no fun or even find it one of the more uncomfortable experiences of your life. To be detached means you know and accept this possibility before you go. Your purpose in going is to improve your love life. This will surely happen, but exactly when it happens and how it happens is for the Universe, or the Higher Spiritual Power, to decide.

The second principle to remember in applying action is the principle of balance. To neglect any level is to diminish your power. Balance is a key to harmonious self-development as well. For example, developing your intellect but ignoring your social skills can have the same effect as building a solid wall between yourself and others, only to leave you wondering why you feel so alone.

Conscious Relating

As has already been discussed, the quality of your experience of a relationship is determined by your relationship skills. I would like to share with you something very powerful. It is a way of applying awareness in relationships which leads to unlimited possibilities.

We learned earlier that every relationship consists of three essential elements: self, other and the relationship between the two. When you direct your awareness to these three factors *while you are relating with the other person*, you will soon realize that you can raise the quality of the relationship and improve the way the relationship functions or affects both of you. The results of applying this simple formula are quite magical. This three-point focus of awareness is a key to tremendous power. As it becomes your habit, all of your relationships will continually improve right before your eyes. At the same time, your awareness in relationships will continually heighten. This means that you will have the ability to direct your creative potential at higher and higher levels, making it possible to bring about higher levels of soulmate harmony in your love life.

This three-point focus is something to be practiced *at all times*, during every moment of relating with another. Practice it intentionally. Remember to check on yourself to be sure you are practicing it while speaking, listening, or simply being in the presence of another. It will gradually free you from having to react automatically, and free you to respond in ways that bring about better and better results.

Here is a brief description of what awareness of each of these points consists of:

1. Awareness of yourself has been discussed earlier. It means noticing what you are saying and how you are saying it. It means observing what you are doing, thinking, and feeling while you are doing, thinking and feeling it.

2. Awareness of the other means that you are paying attention to what he or she is saying and doing. You are observing the reactions of the other to your actions, thoughts, feelings and speech. You are focused on intuitively registering what is happening within the other.

3. Awareness of the relationship means that you are aware of the quality of energy that characterizes the relationship in the moment. Is it romantic? Is it friendly? Is it businesslike? Is it harmonious? Is it chaotic? Is it conflicting? Is it tranquil? Is it intense? Is it sacred? Is it nurturing? Is it strained?

When you are aware of yourself, you will begin to see what you are doing that causes stress, difficulty or unhappiness. You will notice when you have been reacting automatically without remembering to apply this three-point awareness.

When you are aware of the other, you will begin to sense what they need, how you can help, what you can say or do for them and what to avoid for your mutual benefit.

When you focus awareness onto the relationship, you will soon become aware of how you can raise it to a higher level of efficiency, order, beauty and power. You will see what works and what doesn't.

This practice awakens the awareness which guides the intuitive healing process. You will begin to sense, on subtle, inner levels the stress, ease and "dis-ease" in others. You will be able to sense the effects that the relationship between you is having on the other. You will observe the affects upon that other of what you are doing, thinking, feeling and saying. This will alert you to changes and adjustments that you can make to support the natural harmonizing, healing, self-empowering process in the other.

The simple exercise that follows develops the skill of focusing awareness on the three points. Think back to the last encounter you had with another person. It can be as recently as a moment ago, or as far back in your life as you choose.

In your Relationship Journal, make three columns. Label the left-hand column "Self," the middle column "Relationship," and the last column "Other."

In the "Self" column, note something that you said, did, thought or felt while you were with that other.

In the "Other" column, write down something that you observed the other saying, doing, thinking or feeling. Be careful when recording another's thoughts and feelings. You may only be assuming that you know what is going on. Even if the other tells you what he or she has been thinking, all you really know is that he or she *says* that this is the thought or feeling that occurred. This point is important. It has nothing to do with distrust. It is a matter of accuracy, which leads to clearer, sharper, more conscious awareness.

Finally, in the "Relationship" column, describe the quality of your relationship above the apex of the triangle. Was it pleasant, harmonious, intense, friendly, romantic, loving, cold, conflicting, superficial, awkward, combative, easy, difficult? Choose a word or two to describe it.

Self, other and the relationship between are *dynamic*. They are constantly changing. This is why it requires continual awareness focused on the three.

Reviewing your relationships and noting them in your Relationship Journal is a way to develop your awareness in relationships. However, the most effective way is to remember to practice during the day consciously and intentionally at all times during interpersonal encounters. This results in the most rapid progress in raising your level of awareness of the three factors, and developing your ability to direct the forces of your relationships with more creativity, love and intelligence.

Make additional pages in your Relationship Journal to chart other relationships. For example, choose a relationship from your past. It may be interesting to divide your life into three sections of equal times. For example, if you are thirty years old, divide your life into three ten-year periods. If you are sixty, divide it into three twenty-year periods. Then, from each period, recall a relationship encounter and chart it on the triangle.

Purpose In Action

Whenever you apply action aimed at achieving a goal, it will attract to you the opportunities to advance toward that goal. Whatever the immediate effects of your action, the purpose behind it determines its ultimate consequences.

In your Relationship Journal, draw another equilateral triangle. This is the Triangle of Purpose in Action. We can use it to become more aware of our use of the power of action. This will lead to a more purposeful application of that power. Label the top angle "Purpose," the lower left angle "Action," and the right angle "Effects." Below the left angle labeled "Action," write "Mental, Emotional, Physical and Social."

Recall something you have done today. It could be any action at all. When you have thought of it make a note of it under the "Action" angle. Example: "Showered. Ate breakfast."

Above the "Purpose" angle, describe the purpose of your action. What was your aim or objective? What did you hope to accomplish? In the above example, I would write: "Personal hygiene. Nutrition."

Under the "Effects" angle, note one or more of the effects of your action. What actually happened as an immediate consequence? I would write: "Felt clean and refreshed. Felt nourished."

Here is another example. The other day, I called a friend. My purpose was to touch base and keep our connection going. The result of the call was that I left a message on his machine because no one answered.

Sometimes, I find myself surprised by my purpose, or unclear about it. This just occurred in the example of my call to my friend. Until this moment, I had not thought about the purpose consciously. I thought I just wanted to do it. But looking back, my intention became more clear.

The purpose of this exercise is to become more aware of what we are doing, why we are doing it, and what the consequences of our actions are. This expansion of awareness helps us to make more conscious, purposeful choices. It develops a habit of considering what we want to accomplish, and what the probable consequences of our actions will be *before engaging in the act.*

Practicing this exercise regularly helps me to apply it in daily life. When I remember to use it I find that I can avoid many useless actions and reactions on the four lower levels of my power: Mental, Emotional, Physical and Social. It therefore helps me to utilize more of my power to reach my goals.

One of the biggest improvements this has made in my life is in the area of speech. It helped me to realize how much time, attention and energy I used to waste in emotional, pointless, unconscious and automatic speaking.

As I become more aware, I find that I can choose what I say for a conscious purpose, or choose not to say anything because silence, or listening, will work better. In this way I harness the power I used to waste.

Think back now to something that you said to someone recently. Recall a single word or statement and write it under "Action." For instance, this morning I said good morning to my wife.

Above "Purpose," describe what you were trying to accomplish in saying it. In my case, my intention was to support our mutual respect and harmony. (I did not realize that I had this purpose until I reviewed the act just now.)

Below "Effects," describe one or more of the immediate, observable effects of your statement. The effect I observed was increased warmth and intimacy with my wife.

I have noticed that when I use this review exercise after a heated argument, the purpose behind my statements is not really clear. I am not actually sure what it was I was trying to accomplish. When this happens, I usually spend some time thinking about my relationship with that person in order to clearly identify what I feel that I want or need in it.

This Triangle can also be applied with the other levels of our power to act: mental, emotional and social. Let's try it with the social level. Think back to a time when you were with another. It could have been on the telephone or in person. It could have been a client, a business associate, a family member, a friend or your lover. When you recall a time when you were together, write the person's name down under "Action." For instance, I was recently speaking with a friend on the telephone. I would therefore write his name.

Next, write down your purpose in being with them (it could also be a group situation, when you were with more than one person, in which case you would have written a word or two which referred to the group you were with). In my case, my friend returned my call. However, if I was participating in the conversation, I had to have a purpose. Thinking back, my purpose was to show interest in his affairs and to maintain our connection.

Finally, under "Effects," write down one or more of the observable effects of your being with that person or group. In my example, one of the effects was the love I felt for my friend after we talked.

Using this exercise has helped me to recognize individuals whom I feel drained or negative around, and it has generally helped me to recognize the effects of my relationships on subtle levels I used to overlook, but which are nonetheless important. Essentially, it helps me to be more discerning and selective in whom I associate with and when.

Let's now do this for the emotional level. Think back to a time when you were feeling angry, upset, depressed, or happy, exhilarated, inspired. When you think of that time, write down a word or two describing how you felt beneath "Action." For example, I recall a time recently when I felt self-pitying.

Above "Purpose," describe the aim or objective of your emotional reaction or state. What were you attempting to accomplish by feeling that way? (I realize that we do not ordinarily think of having a purpose for our feelings, however, feelings do produce effects; therefore, they are forces which we can harness for the good of ourselves and others). My purpose was to simply express my dissatisfaction.

When I realize my purpose, I can adjust my action. Looking back at the purpose of my self-pity, I am alerted to the fact that there must be something happening in my life I am dissatisfied with. I then apply my thought (mental action) for the purpose of understanding what I want. I use my thought again to determine what would be the best course of action to take for what I want. Having done this, I have turned self-pity into motivation for directed, constructive action and that has raised my spirits.

Finally, under "Effects," write one or more of the consequences you observed as a result of your emotional state. In my case, one effect of my feeling of self-pity was acting as though I was powerless to change things until I realized what I was feeling.

We can also apply this diagram to the mental level of action. Let us do this a little differently. Begin observing your mind. Simply close your eyes and remain alert for the first thought, word or image that crosses your mind. When one occurs (it will probably take about five seconds to realize that one occurred about four seconds ago) write it under "Action." I just did this and one of the thoughts that occurred to me was to wonder where thought comes from.

Above "Purpose," describe the purpose behind the thought. Every thought is stimulated by a motivation, concern or interest. There is always something that we are trying to accomplish in thinking.

Often, it is difficult to know why a thought occurred because the motivation goes by quickly and subtly. Sometimes it seems the thoughts I think are merely conscious echoes of what I just observed or experienced. They seem to flash in my mind for no reason or purpose I can fathom. If you do not know the purpose of a thought, feeling or action, try asking yourself the following question:"Why did I (think, say, feel, do) that?" Give yourself a couple of moments to see if an answer comes. If an answer does not come, leave the space above "Purpose" blank.

Finally, under "Effects," describe one or more of the effects of your thought. In my case, I became aware that I did not know for certain the source of my thoughts. A theory occurred to me, but I do not know if it is merely logical or true. This was not a major issue for me so there was no apparent emotion involved in the effects. However, the effects of the thoughts we think are often a strong emotional reaction, an urge to do or say something, feelings of safety or comfort, etc.

Here is one final use of this diagram for making the most of our power to act with purpose. We can use this diagram to plan future actions. Here is how this can be done for improving our love lives.

In planning, we begin with the top of the triangle. The first step is to clarify purpose. Above "Purpose," write something that you want to accomplish in your love life. If you do not have a specific, definite goal at this moment, you may simply write: "To improve my love life."

Be as deep or as superficial as you like with this stage of the exercise. In fact, when one has not done this before it is often best to start out with something which seems relatively superficial. For instance, you might like it if your mate dressed more sharply when you go out together. Or, you might write that you want to meet the man or woman of your dreams, fall in love, raise a family, and live happily ever after.

In my case, at this time I would like to clarify my focus regarding my relationship. I am not altogether certain of the direction I want things to go. This does not mean anything is wrong, it just means I'm not certain of the future design I want. I describe my purpose as: "To gain clearer focus."

Having written your purpose, consider what action you can take to advance in the direction you want things to go. In other words, think about what you can do for what you want. (Realize that thinking along these lines is already an action, on the mental level, aimed at your advancement toward your goal. However, give yourself a few minutes to come up with something else that you can do.) If, after the end of thinking about it you have no answer, you can write in your space: "To think further on what I can do" or you can write: "To remain open and alert to noticing an idea occurring to me for a purposeful action I can take."

Next, focus on the probable effects of your action. Aside from the fact that it will advance you toward your purpose, are there any other probable consequences you can think of? Do not spend too much time thinking of this unless you feel that it is necessary. If you leave this space blank, return to it after you have done the act you described and then make a note of one or more of the observable effects.

I recommend that you refer to this diagram frequently, every day if possible. It will help you remember to apply all five levels of action purposefully, and to be aware of the immediate effects of your moment-to-moment choices.

Everything we say, think, feel and do uses or applies some measure of our power. The more power we purposefully and deliberately direct, the more progress we will make toward our chosen goals.

Focusing on what you want and applying purposeful action toward bringing it about, directs energy into those purposeful activities. That energy is then unavailable to the negative states. The same principle applies to conflicts in our outer world.

Observe what you are doing to support the conflict. Then, focus on building the conditions that you want in ways that do not involve this conflict.

Let the measure of energy that wants to go into a negative state be the measure of force you send into purposeful action aimed at what you want. This will free you from the negative state and attract the circumstances you are focusing on. It may take a while of building momentum in the purposeful direction of your activities to draw all the energy that habitually flows into the negative reactions. However, with persistence you will win.

Magical Action

You will attract the experience you dedicate your action toward. Your action can be directly related to your goal, or it can be merely symbolic. A symbolic act is something that you do which symbolizes or represents a purposeful function.

When you direct effort into an action for a symbolic purpose, it becomes a magical act. It is magical in the sense that it directs the subconscious and the forces of nature through the invisible implications of the act.

Magical action has been a part of every religion and culture since the beginning of time. Every ceremonial gesture and costume—from drawing an imaginary cross upon your chest to wearing a cap and gown at graduation—is intended to produce a very real change through symbolic motion.

I would like to guide you, step-by-step, in the application of *magical action* in your love life. It does not matter if you are currently in a relationship or not. Using this approach will lead to the continued progress of your relationship experience in the direction of your deepest dreams. Remember once again, however, the very important principle of non-identification. Do not use this or any other exercise with a focus on changing any other person. To break this rule would be to infringe on the free will of others.

Exercise 14: Magical Action

1. Knowing What You Want: In your Relationship Journal, describe what you want in a relationship. Simply make a list of some of the qualities you are looking for in a mate. List one or more qualities for each level of self: physical, emotional, mental, spiritual, social (how your mate or the two of you relate with others). When you write down what you want, be aware that you are making this physical act of writing in order to draw to you the relationship experience you want.

2. Draw a Box: Draw a rectangular box around what you have written. Remember physical effort attracts results.

3. Press Your Palm: Now, place the palm of one of your hands upon what you have written. Imagine that this act of pressing your palm against these words is drawing to you the relationship experience which they represent, the experience you want in the bottom of your heart and the depth of your soul. Know that this act focuses your energy, connecting you with your dreams.

4. Creative Breathing: Now, we will use the breath. Draw in a long, slow breath. Make this breath as slow as you can, let it last as long as possible. Begin with completely empty lungs and, as slowly as possible, fill your lungs to their total capacity. As you do this, keep your palm pressed against your list and imagine your breath is drawing to you the relationship you want.

5. Affirm: Now stand and state the following Kabbalistic Affirmation with your soulmate in mind. Imagine that the act of saying it is drawing the relationship to you in the way the affirmation describes. (Do not state the numbers.)

We are following the path to each other ...
    1. that is true to our highest spiritual potentials
    2. of true wisdom
    3. and understanding
    4. that is truly merciful
    5. and just
    6. that is truly loving and compassionate toward all beings
    7. that is genuinely triumphant and courageous and aligns with our individual goals
    8. that is of utmost honor, self-respect and integrity
    9. that supports our eternal security and stability
    10. that is along the line of our material abundance and physical well-being.

6. Exert: Now you are going to learn how to use the power of exertion in a magical way. Go to a wall in your room. Carefully, and without injuring yourself, push against that wall with all your might. As you do this, imagine that the effort you are making is drawing the relationship experience that you want.

7. Handling: The hands are a symbol of mastery and control, as when you can handle something. Hold your hands cupped before you, as if you were trying to catch rain. Imagine that your ultimate dream of a loving, intimate relationship is right there in your hands. See the dream fitting easily in your palms. As you hold it in your hands, know that you have it in your life. Now, close your hands by pressing the palms flat against each other and imagine that you are pressing the dream relationship into your being and into your life through that action.

8. Stillness: For the next thirty seconds sit absolutely still. Do not permit yourself to make any other movement but breathing. As you make the effort to remain still, concentrate on the fact that you are doing it for the relationship experience you want.

9. Gratitude: Now, for the next thirty seconds imagine the feeling of profound gratitude for being given the relationship experience that satisfies you on every level, fills you with joy, peace and the knowledge that it is good. It may help you to hold your palms together in the prayerful gesture, close your eyes, and focus on the words "thank you."

10. Success: Imagine now that you have all the qualities in a relationship that you want. It is all happening. Consider what you would do next. Once you have achieved this goal, how would you get on with your life? Focus on this for the next thirty seconds.

Magical action may seem silly at first. It forces us to be as a child, trusting, innocent and uninhibited. This can, in itself, be beneficial in relieving our stress and attuning us to the trusting part of ourselves. Magical action sets up an electromagnetic field which draws to you that for which you are acting. It also aligns the body, setting in motion the momentum of constructive action aimed at what you want.

Your phone may not ring the moment you complete your magical action. Your mate may not be totally changed in an instant. What you can count on, however, is the fact that doing things for what you want, even things that only have symbolic value, will and must result in steady improvements in the direction you want things to go. This is cosmic law.

Relying on cosmic law works. When you do not know who or what to trust, you can always turn to the cosmic law of attraction to direct your life.

The Tree of Life Soulmate Chant

Chants have been used for thousands of years to invoke, focus and direct power. On the following page occurs The Tree of Life Soulmate Chant. It is based on the forces represented on the diagram.

The number of each line relates to the corresponding sphere on the diagram. Each sphere represents an essential force or energy in the universe and in ourselves. Those ten essential forces are described by the lines of the chant.

As you recite this chant, concentrate on the relationship experience you want. The chant raises the energy of that union and focuses it into the manifestation process. See and feel the qualities that you are referring to in the chant; be as specific in your visualizing as you can.

The numbers refer to the diagram and are not to be stated.

Tree of Life Soulmate Chant
1. S(he) is spiritual
2. S(he) is wise
3. S(he) is understanding
4. S(he) is trusting and forgiving
5. S(he) is discerning and discriminating
6. S(he) is loving and compassionate
7. S(he) feels triumph in our union
8. S(he) respects herself (or himself)

9. S(he) is sexually satisfied in our union
10. S(he) finds me physically delightful

1. I am one with my spiritual being
2. I am wise
3. I am understanding
4. I am trusting and forgiving
5. I am discerning and discriminating
6. I am loving and compassionate
7. I feel triumph in our union
8. I respect myself
9. I am sexually satisfied in our union
10. I find her (or him) physically delightful

1. We are in spiritual harmony together
2. Together we are wise
3. Together we are understanding
4. Together we are trusting and forgiving
5. Together we are discerning and discriminating
6. Together we are loving and compassionate
7. Together we feel triumph in our union
8. Together we respect ourselves
9. Ours is a sexually satisfying union
10. We find each other physically delightful

As you recite the chant aloud, focus on the reality which the words represent. Recite the chant slowly and clearly, and with an inner certainty that the manifestation of your soulmate relationship is taking place. Once you have read all three parts going down, repeat the chant going from the bottom upward.

You may also choose to recite this chant on tape, with your favorite relaxing music in the background. State it slowly, softly, but clearly over and over for an entire side. The repetition will deepen its effects and help you to remain attuned on deeper and deeper levels to the love life experience that you want. Play the tape when you are relaxing, taking a nap, or going off to sleep at the end of the day. As you hear it, you can either chant along, or simply focus on the experience represented by each line.

Tarot Image 4: The Emperor

We began this chapter with Tarot Image 4: *The Emperor.* This image represents the organizing power of consciousness which brings things together for a useful purpose.

The water streaming through the picture represents the stream of creative imagination that has been stimulated into fruitful activity. As these images proliferate, they are organized and systematized to constitute reality in line with the Cosmic Plan of Higher Mind.

The glacial ice-structures above the moving stream symbolize the crystallization of ideas, schemes and concepts into thought structures that make sense. This Tarot image also represents the rational mind. The function of this mind is to guide the creative imagination into a logical, systematic arrangement which we can follow with action to achieve an objective.

There are two symbols of the astrological sign of Aries in this image: the emblem on the Emperor's helmet and the lamb pictured on the arms of the throne supporting him. The sign of Aries represents the rulership of activity, and is associated anatomically with the head of the human body. This suggests that The Emperor is the head or ruler of action in line with the Logos or True Reason behind existence.

By meditating on this image, your subconscious is directed to alert your conscious mind to carefully oversee the activities of your imagination. It also strengthens your ability to reason. As you focus on this image, any excess energy that is going into the emotions will be redirected to the mind for clear, sharp thinking.

Focusing on this image will align your activities with the Cosmic Plan. It will also empower your ability to plan intelligent strategies and to organize your inner and outer activities.

Exercise 15: The Emperor

1. Take three slow, gentle, full breaths. Enter the state of focused relaxation known as *attention without tension.*

2. Meditate on Tarot Image 4 for one to three minutes. Feel the image entering you through your attention and impressing itself on the core of your being. Imagine the picture is teaching you how to reason and organize as it aligns your inner and outer activities with the Cosmic Plan.

3. State the following slowly and clearly with attention ready to recognize the reality which the words describe: "My reasoning is clear, and my inner and outer activities are aligned with the Cosmic Plan."

Having stated this affirmation, know that The Emperor within you must and will respond by ordering your consciousness so that you not only see your life plan clearly, but also feel yourself traveling along it.

Tarot Image 6: The Lovers

7

Be True To Yourself

Angel was crying after attending her younger sister's wedding, but they were tears of pain, not joy. She was angry with herself for being envious. Her sister was nearly ten years younger then herself and already married. Angel had never even been engaged.

She drove her four-wheel drive vehicle deep into the woods along a dirt road, parked, and walked toward the base of Mount Wheeler which towered thirteen thousand feet into the clouds. She walked up the mild grade and then started her climb along the rugged trail. Her objective was to somehow lose her pain and find an answer to a question she could not articulate.

Along one of the switchbacks, she came upon an elderly, gray-haired man who sat upon a boulder, apparently resting. He introduced himself as Ralph.

"You're not here on your own, are you?" Angel asked the old man.

"No," said Ralph. "My group's up ahead. This is where I belong. This is the top of my mountain."

There was something about him that held Angel there. When she began to move on, she stopped as though a magnetic force drew her back.

"I can see you are hurting," Ralph said. "What's the problem?"

Angel looked at him strangely. It was unusual for her to talk about her problems with anyone, let alone a complete stranger. But perhaps because she felt at the end of her rope, perhaps because this *was* such a perfect stranger, she found herself pouring out her story.

When her story was through, Ralph responded. "Your True Self is your eternal, spiritual nature. It is like the pattern in a seed which guides its growth process, as well as the power within it to grow to its full potential. Read the Bhagavad Gita and realize that *you* are Krishna. Read the Psalms of the Old Testament and realize that *you* are the Creator. All religions are aimed at guiding and leading the individual into the conscious realization of the infinite I Am.

"Your True Self attracts the experiences that it needs to grow. You can also attract your destiny through purposeful action and creative imagination. When you know or imagine what you want, and do things for it, you draw what you want to you.

"Direct your life by designing in imagination the conditions that you want and do what you can to reach your goals. Find peace and security with conditions beyond your control by trusting that your True Self is drawing to itself the experiences that it needs for its next step in real advancement."

Angel smiled. She did not know what to think. "You talk about life as if it were a science. You make it sound so simple."

Ralph laughed. "I doubt it. That's just all I know."

His group approached and he joined them on their way down. Angel continued sitting on the rock, thinking of what the strange man had said: "This is where I belong. This is the top of my mountain."

The True Self Tree Exercise

The only way to experience more love, peace, joy and security in life is by aligning with your True Self. No other relationship can replace inner conflict with harmony.

Harmonious, loving relationships increase the power of those in them. Two individuals working in harmony can accomplish more together than separately. As each considers, respects and coordinates with the other, both are empowered to express and achieve their best.

Our desire for the higher levels of Self translates into a desire to find our soulmate. However, a relationship in turmoil can be one of the most painful experiences in life and hurl us into our lowest self expression. Every condition will eventually be followed by its opposite. Ignorant of this law of opposites, we look for a relationship that is problem free, without any hope of finding one.

Intimate relationships are not sources of growth—they are extremely powerful opportunities for growth. The energy released by an intimate relationship can deepen your awareness and release your greater potential. This gives us the sense of fulfilling our life purpose but you do not need an intimate, romantic relationship to fulfill your life's purpose. We evolve naturally. Every situation is an experience in the growth process. We have all we need to grow.

Your True Self is constantly learning and growing. The growth process is represented by the **Kabbalah Tree of Life** diagram. Each sphere represents a development direction accomplished by every experience. A meditation on the Tree of Life diagram acts as a reminder of the growth process and helps us cooperate with it more freely.

These are the ten essential qualities of Higher Self Expression:
Sphere 1: The Spiritual energy or point of pure, focused power to be:
Sphere 2: Wise;
Sphere 3: Understanding;
Sphere 4: Merciful, trusting and forgiving;
Sphere 5: Just and able to make sacrifices for a higher gain;
Sphere 6: Compassionate, loving and balanced;
Sphere 7: Courageous and confident;
Sphere 8: Respectful of all beings;
Sphere 9: Eternally strong and stable in Higher Self expression;
Sphere 10: In all material plane circumstances (through the experiences of birth, life and death in the physical body).

Exercise 16: Tree of Life Exercise

1. Take three slow, gentle, full breaths and enter the state of focused relaxation known as *attention without tension.*

2. Look at the Tree of Life diagram for one to three minutes. Imagine that its pattern is the actual pattern of your innermost core. As you view it, also imagine that this pattern is aligning you through your subconscious with the true pattern and purpose of your innermost self.

3. Place one finger on Sphere 1 and state the following: "I am one with the point of pure spiritual power to be:"

4. Place your finger on Sphere 2 and state: "Wise."

5. Place your finger on Sphere 3 and state: "Understanding."

6. Place your finger on Sphere 4 and state: "Merciful, trusting and forgiving."

7. Place your finger on Sphere 5 and state: "Just."

8. Place your finger on Sphere 6 and state: "Balanced, loving and compassionate toward all beings."

9. Place your finger on Sphere 7 and state: "Courageous and confident."

10. Place your finger on Sphere 8 and state: "Respectful of all beings."

11. Place your finger on Sphere 9 and state: "Stable in Higher Self expression"

12. Place your finger on Sphere 10 and state: "Through all experiences, including physical."
    You have now completed the exercise. Know that what you have said is so.

Your Most Important Relationship

Acceptance of *what is*, is one of the ways your True Self receives more of the energy of your current experience and advances in its eternal, evolutionary process. Your True Self attracts the experiences that it needs. Your complete surrender to this process will bring you all the peace, love, joy, security and power *you* need.

The natural order process of evolution is automatic and ongoing. There is nothing that you or I can do to stop it. As we learn to accept and to trust this process, we discover the genuine peace, love, harmony and security that we have been seeking.

The difficulty in this surrender is that the True Self is not concerned with our personal desires, likes, dislikes, attachments and aversions. It is often necessary to experience circumstances that we want to escape or avoid with all our might. When this is happening, we have a fundamental choice to make.

When life forces you to embrace the intolerable you can allow yourself to be changed, to release your aversions and replace your attachments with trust in the larger process going on. In making this choice, you enter what the ancient mystics referred to as *The Path*, which leads straight to the higher states of consciousness rather than detouring through resistance and fear.

If you choose to hold onto your attachments and condemn circumstances you are fighting a futile war. The lesson we all learn from this again and again is that it is an utter waste. At the end of every cycle of pain, loss or difficulty comes a cycle of freedom and attainment that more than compensates for what we have endured.

You can either trust life or fear life. No relationship can protect us from the cosmic process, the onward march of our evolution, or the alternating high and low cycles of life. An intimate relationship merely brings the process to a higher pitch of energy.

Your evolution into higher levels of power for greater self-expression is a natural process following natural laws. One of these is "The Law of Increasing Power." This Law states that as you align with your True Self, more power is released for you to handle. Each set of circumstances in which you find yourself is essentially a dynamic energy system. To the degree that you

remain balanced and true to your Self in your present circumstances, you will find yourself in an even more powerful situation next time. Increased power will then be available for you
to broaden your True Self expression, and thus the evolutionary
process advances.

Being in a relationship does not save us from the weaknesses
or imbalances which make being alone unbearable yet make
relationships a hell. Our ability to be content, secure and true to
our Higher Self will be tested by every experience in life. As we
learn to accept this process and trust in it, we discover that the
most important relationship is between us and ourselves.

Exercise 17: Developing Trust and Cooperation
With Your True Self:

1. Take three slow, gentle, full breaths.

2. Imagine now a seed of light in the core of your being. It was
   placed there when the universe began, at the dawn of time.
   Imagine yourself looking down into your chest where you see
   this softly glowing seed of light. Let the color of the light be
   whatever color it wants to be, let it shift and change colors as
   its color is an expression of your unique energy growing. As
   you watch the light within you, know that it is your True Being.

3. As you continue to look at this glowing seed, the outer shell of
   light becomes transparent and you can see into it. You see
   streams and patterns of fine lines of light in its interior. These
   lines are the seed's pattern which determines your lines of
   development through eternity. Your destiny is written in those
   lines of pure light. You now see a deeper glow. It is the glow of
   your divine potential, the destined fruit of the seed of light.

4. Permit the image of the seed of light to pass, replaced by an
   inner *feel* of the lines of your True Self's destiny. Breathe in a
   long, slow breath and as you do, imagine that you are completely one with the feeling of those lines, guiding you along
   your True Path.

5. Now, state the following affirmation, with attention focused on
   the experience which the words describe: "I and my True Self
   are now One."

Spiritual Romance

Alex felt the pressure to be both a playboy and a stable, devoted family man. A "real man," his emotions told him, must be both. Because this is impossible, Alex could neither accept himself nor allow a relationship to become "too" intimate.

Whenever a relationship progressed into increasing involvement, Alex became more cold, aloof and resistant. He feared that if his love partner got too close, he would become emotionally trapped and unable to fulfill the other responsibility of "real manhood." Eventually, he would leave the relationship and return to playing the field in the quest of another victory.

But leaving, however, left him feeling terribly guilty and ashamed. It was not unusual for Alex to experience impotence during the "fun" of a one night stand or superficial fling, which was something he never experienced in a serious relationship.

As he entered the "playboy" circuit, the "family man" urge haunted him. He felt terrible about leaving the woman who loved him, terrible about himself.

When he'd had enough of this suffering, he decided there must be a deeper level to himself than these superficial programs of "real manhood" that were impossible to live up to. There had to be an inner guidance system he could follow which would lead him to greater happiness instead of his recurring pain. He was currently in a relationship with a woman named Katherine, and the urge to leave was growing stronger. Instead of being run by that urge, he now observed it without identifying with it. He accepted that there was a higher force guiding and directing his destiny and trusted that it knew what was best for him. He regarded his urge to escape intimacy as his personal ego which, he had learned, always seemed to lead him down a dead-end street.

Rather than trying to make things happen, he practiced trusting that what he needed to happen would occur. When Katherine insisted on more romance and more commitment, he observed his fear and inner resistance. He wanted to run but did not. He simply said he was giving all that he could right now. This, at least, was an improvement upon his old pattern which would have been to move further away from her.

Katherine was patient but insisted on understanding his process. He explained his old pattern and that he was working on breaking it. This touched her heart as it revealed to her a deeper side of his nature than she had guessed was there.

Over the next six months Alex continued working on aligning with his deeper self. Their relationship gradually changed from one of romance to friendship. Katherine genuinely liked him and respected his efforts toward growth. He loved sharing his insights and discoveries with her. They read together, attended classes, went to spiritual retreats separately and together. They followed the devotional path toward the illumination of the Self which mystics through the ages have explored.

The quest for the True Self within became the strongest link between them. That spiritual foundation was deeper and stronger than the earlier patterns which had kept Alex from progressing into deeper intimacy.

One day he realized that he was falling in love with Katherine on a deeper level than he had ever known before. Slowly, their relationship evolved into a journey that was more exciting, romantic and honest than either of them had dreamed possible.

Tarot Image 6: The Lovers

We began this chapter with Tarot Image 6: *The Lovers*. It represents the three levels of mind working together in harmony: the conscious, the subconscious and the superconscious, which is the Higher Mind of the True Self.

The male represents the conscious mind. This is the mind that sees out into the world, observes what is happening in the present and sends the information it receives to the subconscious mind for processing. The conscious mind is associated with male energy because looking out is an expression of outflowing force.

The female represents the subconscious mind. The subconscious receives the impressions through the conscious mind and determines the appropriate response. It is associated with a female because it receives from the male and gives birth to a response which is the product of their union.

The female in the image is looking up at the Archangel Michael, representative of True Self. The hands of the True Self suggest the pose of a protector, provider and guide. The female's upward gaze and receptive stance demonstrate her complete and utter trust in the Higher Power, which is always at work in our lives.

The male suggests that you apply your conscious awareness to be on the alert for personal, ego-based drives, desires and attachments. When you notice these, become as the female in the picture—surrender to the Higher Self's goals for you. This process of turning over your energy to the Higher Self may seem unclear to you. That is what the cloud in the image represents. However, by meditating on this image, you are subconsciously instructed in this process.

Exercise 18: The Lovers

1. Take three slow, gentle, full breaths.

2. Meditate on Tarot Image 6 for one to three minutes. Feel the image impressing itself on the core of your being. Imagine the picture teaching you to direct your power of conscious control with trust in the Higher Power for reaching your ultimate potential and fulfilling your life purpose.

3. State the following slowly and clearly with attention ready to recognize the reality which the words describe: "My conscious and subconscious are wholly aligned with my superconscious mind."

   Having stated this affirmation, know that your conscious and subconscious minds, The Lovers within, are working together to give birth to your Higher Self.

AFTERWORD ━━━━━━━━

Mystics through the ages have taught that as we purify our own consciousness, we make the greatest contribution possible to the rest of humanity and to the planet as a whole. The love and balance within you radiates and is absorbed by all. Even the plants are nurtured by your love.

As you free yourself of the inner chains holding you back, you weaken the chains binding us all. As you develop the strength to handle whatever life gives to you with peace, poise and dedication to your beliefs, every other human soul is strengthened to express and experience the same.

Self-work is not selfish. Focusing on self-development is like an artist focusing on a work of beauty. The more loving, wise and courageous you are, the more of those qualities you share.

Accept your greatest trials and most difficult troubles as opportunities to help us all. The more love, wisdom and balance you radiate in the midst of these experiences, the freer each of us becomes to experience those higher levels of consciousness during our darker hours as well. Mystics refer to work on self-development as the *Secret Path* because your efforts are within you and the help you bring to humanity is also within. To tread the *Secret Path* just might be the greatest act of love of which one is capable.

Your efforts to liberate yourself for soulmate love frees each one of us to know the joy of that love in our own experience. Perhaps we should refer to those who do this inner work as *Soulmate Warriors*; they are certainly heroes of the heart.

Bob Lancer is the author of several books in the field of spiritual growth and mystical studies. He also invented the Kabbalah Cards for awakening higher consciousness and receiving intuitive insight. He offers individual counseling and instruction, and also presents talks, workshops and seminars. He may be contacted at Tools of the Tree, P. O. Box 416, Lake Forest, IL 60045.

Write for a free copy of *Master of Life WINNERS* magazine. It contains news and articles on the subjects of metaphysics, psychic exploration and self-help, in addition to complete information on all Sutphen Seminars, and over 350 self-help and self-exploration audio and video tapes from Valley of the Sun Publishing: hypnosis, meditation, sleep programming, subliminal programming, and New Age music. A sampling of some of our audio and video tapes on love and relationships are contained on the following pages.

Valley of the Sun Publishing
Box 3004, Agoura Hills, CA 91376
Phone: 818/889-1575

VALLEY OF THE SUN

ATTRACTING LOVE
Drawing Your Soulmate To You
Video Hypnosis®

If you're ready for the truly loving experience of a soulmate relationship, use this 30-minute video tape to draw this person to you.

Video Hypnosis® combines two kinds of hypnosis (verbal and visual) with two kinds of subliminals (flashed on the screen and embedded into the background music). The result? Ultra-powerful programming. These tapes program both the conscious and the subconscious mind with new beliefs. Beliefs generate thoughts and emotions, which create experiences. Change those beliefs and you change your life. **30 minutes/VHS only.**

Examples of Suggestions

You are ready to give and receive unconditional love. ■ You are ready for a warm primary relationship. ■ You draw the lover who is right for you into your life now. ■ A warm fulfilling soulmate relationship now manifests in your life. ■ You draw your lover to you.

.... VHS110–$19.95

ATTRACTING PERFECT LOVE
RX17® Digital 3-D Audio Tape

RX17® tapes combine state-of-the-art recording and leading edge brain/mind technology to synchronize left and right brain. You are then receptive to new beliefs. Beliefs generate thoughts and emotions, which create experiences. To change your life, you must change your beliefs.

Side A: Alpha Level programming: A soothing voice is combined with environmental sounds, relaxing you while you imagine a peaceful tropical island. **Side B:** The suggestions are embedded into 30 minutes of soothing stereo music.

Example of Suggestions:

You now create the space in your life for the perfect love relationship. ■ You are now ready to meet the perfect lover. ■ You project warmth and openness. ■ You are ready to give and receive unconditional love. ■ You now focus the power of your subconscious mind upon drawing the perfect lover into your life.

.... RX102–$12.50

LOVE & RELATIONSHIP
AUDIO/VIDEO TAPES

ATTRACT LOVE & CREATE A SUCCESSFUL RELATIONSHIP
5-Tape Audio/Video Mind Power Programming Album

This album helps you attract love and create a successful relationship.

1. Attracting Love Video Hypnosis®: VHS–30 minutes. **Examples of Suggestions:** You are now open to the experience of a loving relationship. ■ You are ready for a warm, fulfilling relationship. ■ You now draw the appropriate lover into your life. ■ You now create a loving relationship of trust and shared goals.

2. Instruction/Motivation Tape.

3. The 25 Best Ways To Find Love & Make It Work: Side A is a condensed examination of the 25 most powerful, proven ideas on the subject. Side B is **Goal Imprinting**.

4. Attracting Perfect Love: Side A: RX17® Alpha Level programming; Side B: Soothing music with subliminal suggestions. 60 minutes.

5. Charisma (Drawing People To You): Side A: RX17® Alpha Level programming; Side B: Music with subliminal suggestions. 60 minutes.

.... PK107–$59.95

RELATIONSHIP IMPROVEMENT
Probe 7® Audio Tape

Probe 7® is a unique kind of 21st-century brain/mind programming using three-dimensional sound to relax you by synchronizing both brain hemispheres.

There is no verbal induction but the follow-response cycle-per-second effects generate an eyes-open, light-level, altered state conducive to accepting suggestions. Use the tapes while doing routine tasks, while going to sleep, or as an altered-state tape. (Don't use while driving, operating equipment or doing anything requiring real concentration.)

Example of Suggestions

Your relationship gets better and better. ■ You openly communicate and share yourself. ■ You totally commit to your relationship and support your lover in ways that increase self-esteem. You do. ■ You experience aliveness, excitement, joy, and pleasure in your relationship. ■ You now communicate directly, honestly and easily with your lover.

.... P103–$14.95

You May Call Toll-Free To Order With VISA or MasterCard: 1-800-421-6603

ATTRACTING THE RIGHT LOVE RELATIONSHIP
2-Tape Album

If you are really serious about finding a mate, this album will assist you to accomplish your desires.

Tape 1: Overcoming The Inability To Have A Relationship Hypnosis–Alternate this tape with tape 3; Tape 2: Sleep Programming; Tape 3: Attracting Love Hypnosis; Tape 4: Subliminal Suggestions/Charisma.

Suggestion Examples: You project an inner warmth and charisma that attracts others. ■ You project self-confidence and independence.

2 tapes and Instruction Manual.

.... C838–$24.95

SOULMATES
2-Tape Album

Do you want to meet your Twin Soul, the perfect partner for you? Once together, you usually experience a lifelong relationship that allows you to accomplish soul goals.

Tape 1: Finding Your Soulmate–A higher-self, deep-level meditation session. Tape 2: Soulmate Verification–Check out potential soulmates. Tapes 3 & 4: Subliminal Suggestions.

Suggestion examples: You are now open and ready for a twin-soul relationship. ■ You call down the Power of Powers and draw your soulmate to you. ■ You are ready to give and receive with total commitment.

2 tapes and Instruction Manual.

.... C835–$24.95

THE 25 BEST WAYS TO IMPROVE YOUR LOVE LIFE
Audio Cassette

Although there is no one formula for improving your love life, the behavioral experts continue to prove that there are several factors that contribute most to enhancing sex and your love relationship.

Side A: The Very Latest Information—The life-changing advice on Side A examines the most powerful, proven ideas on the subject.

Side B: Bi-Level Goal Imprinting —Play this side anywhere, while driving or doing other things. Also, use Side B as ultra-powerful **Sleep Programming.** Instructions for using Side B provided at the end of Side A.

.... E107–$9.98

THE 25 BEST WAYS TO FIND LOVE & CREATE A SUCCESSFUL RELATIONSHIP
Audio Cassette

Do you know what you are looking for in a relationship? Unique ideas on how to find the right lover and advice from the behavioral experts on how to create a successful relationship once you do. Side A offers the 25 most powerful, proven findings on relationships and covers critically important information you probably aren't aware of. Side B helps you program the suggestions into reality.

.... E112–$9.98

MAKE CHECKS PAYABLE TO
Valley of the Sun Publishing
Box 3004, Agoura Hills, CA 91376
818/889-1575

ORDER
FORM
SM2

Name

Address

City   State   Zip

Item Number	Name of Item	Qty.	Price

NO CASH OR C.O.D.'S PLEASE

Prices subject to change without notice. Offers in other Valley of the Sun catalogs do not relate to any items offered here. VISA and MasterCard orders, call toll-free: 1-800-421-6603.

CANADIAN—Please include $7.50 extra in U.S. funds.
FOREIGN—Please write for a PRO FORMA invoice.

MERCHANDISE TOTAL	
CA SALES TAX (Residents only 8.25%)	
SHIPPING CHARGE	$3.00
ORDER TOTAL	

MAKE CHECKS PAYABLE TO
Valley of the Sun Publishing
Box 3004, Agoura Hills, CA 91376
818/889-1575

ORDER
FORM
SM2

Name

Address

City   State   Zip

Item Number	Name of Item	Qty.	Price

NO CASH OR C.O.D.'S PLEASE

Prices subject to change without notice. Offers in other Valley of the Sun catalogs do not relate to any items offered here. VISA and MasterCard orders, call toll-free: 1-800-421-6603.

CANADIAN—Please include $7.50 extra in U.S. funds.
FOREIGN—Please write for a PRO FORMA invoice.

MERCHANDISE TOTAL	
CA SALES TAX (Residents only 8.25%)	
SHIPPING CHARGE	$3.00
ORDER TOTAL